Tiny Tales

mini saga competition
for Primary Schools from Young Writers

Southern England

First published in Great Britain in 2007 by
Young Writers, Remus House, Coltsfoot Drive,
Peterborough, PE2 9JX
Tel (01733) 890066 Fax (01733) 313524
All Rights Reserved

© Copyright Contributors 2007
SB ISBN 978-1-84431-340-2

Disclaimer
Young Writers has maintained every effort
to publish stories that will not cause offence.
Any stories, events or activities relating to individuals
should be read as fictional pieces and not construed
as real-life character portrayal.

Foreword

Young Writers was established in 1991, with the aim of encouraging the children and young adults of today to think and write creatively. Our latest primary school competition, *Tiny Tales*, posed an exciting challenge for these young authors: to write, in no more than fifty words, a story encompassing a beginning, a middle and an end. We call this the mini saga.

Tiny Tales Southern England is our latest offering from the wealth of young talent that has mastered this incredibly challenging form. With such an abundance of imagination, humour and ability evident in such a wide variety of stories, these young writers cannot fail to enthral and excite with every tale.

Contents

Cadland Primary School, Holbury
Elizabeth Drake (10) 13
Chloe Dickens (10) 14
Emily Kate Sharpe (10) 15
Jacqueline Rice (10) 16
Hannah Smith (10) 17
Sophie Canton (9) 18
Daisy Price (9) 19
Chloe Argent (9) 20
Ryan Harris (10) 21
Daniel Sharp (10) 22

Cottesmore St Mary's RC School, Hove
Alisha Carrigan (10) 23
Hannah Donaghy (10) 24
Bethan Clark (10) 25

Harlands Primary School, Uckfield
Madeleine Hanford (10) 26
George Reed (10) 27
Emily Muxworthy (9) 28
Kitty Ziolek (10) 29
Anastasia Hiscox (8) 30
Aoife McManus (9) 31
Ellie Tew (11) 32
Lily Wanless (8) 33
Darcy Brown (7) 34

Robert Miller (10) 35
Charlie Tatnall (9) 36

Highfield CE Primary School, Southampton
Sarah Romilly (11) 37
Ivan Zheludev (11) 38
Cleome Rawnsley (10) 39
Tina Wu (11) 40
Zenobia Summers (11) 41
Joseph D'Souza (11) 42
Natalie Ertl (11) 43
Ramzan Bilal (11) 44
Reuben Vulliamy (11) 45
Christie Arnold (11) 46
Jasmeet Khalsa (11) 47
Freddie Chart (11) 48
Hugo Wolfe (11) 49
Matt Mors (11) 50

Icklesham CE Primary School, Icklesham
Summer Brighton (8) 51

Kings Copse Primary School, Southampton

Georgia Dalley (8) 52
Nick Roberts (10) 53
Dylan Thorpe (10) 54
Emma Green (10) 55
Holly (10) 56
Sommer Ledger (9) 57
Ailish Setford (10) 58
Alex Dallimore (10) 59
Megan Williams (10) 60
Charlotte Lewis 61
Peter Kidd (8) 62
Lauren Merritt (8) 63
William Churcher (8) 64
Sherrie Hall (8) 65
Samantha Marsh (7) 66
Emily Sprenger (7) 67
Carys Cotton (8) 68
Joseph Harding (8) 69
Rory Clarke (9) 70
Celest Dring (9) 71
George Wright (9) 72
Katie Dalmas (9) 73
Elliott Prince (9) 74
Thomas Edwards (9) 75
George Gough (9) 76
Jeff Damerell (9) 77
Annabelle Ede (8) 78
Nathaniel O'Horan (9) 79
Charlie Conlon (10) 80

Katy Conlon (8) 81
Jonathan Guy (9) 82

Our Lady of Lourdes RC Primary School, Rottingdean

Alex Papanicolaou (8) 83
George Turner (8) 84
Grace Walker (9) 85
Jack Dunsmore (9) 86
Thomas Greenstein (10) 87
Juliet Maxted (9) 88
Alex Maxted (9) 89

St Alban's CE(A) Primary School, Havant

Kezia Quarrie-Jones (8) 90
Imogen Walsh (8) 91
Emily Frost (8) 92
Alice Kaminski (8) 93
Joanne Marshall 94
Georgina Mellor (9) 95
Katie Gould (10) 96
Madeleine Spice (9) 97
Nicholas Robertson (9) 98
Daniel Mann (10) 99
Mollie Griffiths (9) 100
Johanna Horsman (9) 101
Amy Frost (9) 102
Matthew Lee (9) 103
Euan Langford 104
Georgina Mason (8) 105

Chloe Anderson (8)	106
Daniel Aspey (9)	107
Liam Thomas (10)	108
Joseph Walsh (9)	109
Hannah Aspley (10)	110
Amy Shepherd (9)	111
Alicia Carpenter (10)	112
Alfie Simms (8)	113
Holly Horn (8)	114

St Joseph's RC Primary School, Christchurch

Laurie Harman (11)	115
Pierre Cochart (10)	116
Reuben King (11)	117
Jack Myers (11)	118
Seana Morrison (11)	119
Natalie Dunn (11)	120
Amelia Butt (11)	121
Molly Board (11)	122
Daniel Churchill (11)	123
Bradley Ford (11)	124
Sophie Livsey (11)	125
James Wheeler (10)	126
Anna Davies (10)	127
Elysha Riordan (11)	128
Alice Marshall (11)	129
Soniya Santhosh (11)	130
Bethany Tyler (11)	131
Jacob Knight (10)	132
Thomas Finch (11)	133

St Jude's RC Primary School, Fareham

Lois Bell (10)	134
Molly Hamilton (10)	135
Lauren Brown (10)	136
Cameron Smith (10)	137
Martha North (10)	138
Grace Baggott (10)	139
Caroline Duff (10)	140
Adam Deary (10)	141
Stuart Nixon (9)	142
Oliver Pegrum (10)	143
Liam Perella (10)	144
Christopher Lowman (10)	145

Southway Junior School, Burgess Hill

Jodie Harrison (10)	146
Satya Ramkissun (9)	147
Ellen Shaw (9)	148
Amie Tidd (9)	149
Joshua Brown (9)	150
Eithan-James Smith (8)	151
Phoebe Turner (10)	152
Miranda Hart (9)	153
Alex Faria (10)	154
Shannon Paulsen (10)	155
Alice Dawes (10)	156
Jennifer David (10)	157
Sam Gething (10)	158
Bethany Cox (10)	159

Rebecca Davess (10)	160
Sally Gardiner (9)	161
Imogen Wilson (10)	162
Tom Jenkins (10)	163
Matthew Carpenter (11)	164
Jacob Instone-Brewer (11)	165
Austin Golding (11)	166
Ben McCreadie (10)	167
Connie Pattison (11)	168
Luke Wilson (11)	169
Kate Abercromby (10)	170
Claire Oldacre (10)	171
Aby Blake (11)	172
Lucy Bennet (11)	173
Chloe Woodall (11)	174
Scarlett Secrett (9)	175
Lewis Pontremoli (9)	176
Elizabeth Noble (8)	177
Matthew Thoburn (9)	178
Hayley Richardson (9)	179
Sam Griffin (9)	180
Ellie Hopwood (9)	181
Jason Barrett (9)	182
Rachel Carter (9)	183
Vicky Lee (10)	184
Charlie Jones (10)	185
Anna-Louise Harris (10)	186
Georgia Holloway (10)	187
Isabel Trott (9)	188
Alex Gregory (10)	189
Ellie Powell (10)	190
Tommy King (10)	191
Harry Woolven (9)	192
Molly Dennett-Thorpe (8)	193
Sarah Owen (9)	194
George Brown	195
Isobel Penfold (8)	196
Ryan Sandall (9)	197
Emily Baxter (9)	198
Emily Sayers (9)	199
Leah Walden (9)	200
Julia Phillips (11)	201
Jessica Manley (11)	202
Shannon Webb (11)	203
Katherine Roberts	204
Alexandra Pattenden (10)	205
Connor Glaze (11)	206
Lewis Walker (11)	207
Maria Romer (11)	208
Kathryn Tidbury	209
Georgia Vigar (8)	210
Lucy Jellett (8)	211
Shannon Smith (7)	212
Sam Rattle (8)	213
Saffron Revell (8)	214
Jamie Bareham (8)	215
Cameron Beattie (8)	216
Ellie Scott (8)	217
Parmila Manan	218
George Clare (9)	219
Courtney Hartfield (9)	220
Michaela Cartwright-Ormston (9)	221

Sophie Ackland (9) 222
Leah Batson Jenner (9) 223
Georgina Owen (8) 224
Ellie Parker (10) 225
Charlotte Bates (9) 226
Benjamin House (9) 227
David Sadler (9) 228

Talavera Junior School, Aldershot
Jude Michie (9)......................................229
Katie Robson (7) 230
Bindu Thapa (8).....................................231
Kiya Brown (8) 232
Lloyd McCarthy (9) 233
Ben Colvin (8) 234
Thomas Askey (8) 235
Annie Davies (8) 236
Billy Gilfilan (8) 237
Abigail Smith (8) 238
Tyler Duckworth (9)................................239
Samuel Cresswell (9) 240
Amy Rose (9)...241
Thomas Clarkson (7).............................242
Brendan Kane (8) 243
Alex Laken (8)..244
Joseph Rowles (9) 245
Nicole Oakley (9) 246
Yetnam Limbu (8) 247
Leena Cobb (9) 248
Billie-Jo Churm (8).................................249
Lewis Totterdell (8).................................250

Millie Thomas (7)....................................251
Callum Waters (8)...................................252
Diya Gurung (8)......................................253

Velmead Junior School, Fleet
Harry Prescott (8) 254
Neve Mills (8)...255
Lauren Pocock (8) 256
Abigail Larkin (8) 257
Louise King (8) 258
Peter Wilkins..259
Jack Pearce (8) 260
Ella Hurst (8) 261
Jake Wish (8)...262
Sophie Hayes (8)...................................263
Scott Newstead (7)................................264
Jessica Staker (8)..................................265
Simon Malley (8) 266
Victoria Driscoll (8) 267
Miles Wheway (9)..................................268
Kailey Driscoll (9)...................................269
Christopher Altini (9)..............................270
Ross Newman (9)..................................271
Matthew Lockett (9)...............................272
Isobel Dudfield (9)..................................273
Olivia Close (10) 274
Callum Gooding (8)................................275
Brittany Pepper......................................276
Alexander Medler 277
Dominic Abbott 278
Will Jones (10).......................................279

Emma Harber (10) 280
James Galbraith (11)..............................281
Adam Russell (11)..................................282
Phillip Chorlton (11)................................283
Vrushangan Sumanoharan (11)..............284
Andrea Goring (11) 285
Robert Snellock (11)...............................286
Tom Goodyear (10) 287
Alexandra Keenan (11)...........................288
Nadia Hamid (11) 289
Michael Robinson (11) 290
James Leggett (11).................................291
Thomas Bee (11).....................................292
Jamie Richards (11) 293
Jarvis Reay (11).......................................294

West Dean CE Primary School, Chichester
Jolyon Dannatt (10).................................295
Robert McCann (11)................................296
Theo Ormrod Davis (10) 297
Ella Herman (9) 298
Ollie Dodge (9)..299
Freya Davies (11) 300
Bethan Jerrett (11)...................................301
Louise Cresswell (8)................................302
Rebecca Callow (10)...............................303
Esther King (11) 304
Hannah Lyons (10)..................................305
Luke Ewins (9)...306

The Mini Sagas

Untitled

It was tight shut. The door wouldn't budge. I didn't know who or what was in the room with me. I reached for the torch, it was put in my hand. I turned and frantically pulled at the door. I wish my little brother wouldn't lock me in my room.

Elizabeth Drake (10)
Cadland Primary School, Holbury

Untitled

Once a princess dropped her golden ball in a pond, a toad called Albert saw this happen so he jumped in and grabbed the shimmering ball. He jumped out and the princess gave him a big slobbery kiss. He turned into a prince and they both lived happily ever after.

Chloe Dickens (10)
Cadland Primary School, Holbury

The Magic Spell And A Rabbit

Rebecca was sat on a rock practising her spells. A rabbit hopped by. She turned it into a bat, then into a flower. A few minutes later she turned it into a monster, when she was meant to turn it back into a rabbit. She ran. The monster hugged her.

Emily Kate Sharpe (10)
Cadland Primary School, Holbury

The Strange Appearance

I was walking to the park. I was opening the gate. I was running around madly. I was playing with my friends. I was chatting, they all said the same thing. They said that they didn't believe in vampires. Then, all of a sudden ... *Dracula appeared.*

Jacqueline Rice (10)
Cadland Primary School, Holbury

My Love Forever!

I loved it before, I love it today, I'll love it forever, don't stand in my way. I'm running so far, so frustrating still, I've been poisoned with a love pill. My heart's still beating, I'm alive still, oh no, I've eaten all the chocolate!

Hannah Smith (10)
Cadland Primary School, Holbury

Little Red Riding Hood

Once a girl called Red Riding Hood was visiting her granny who was ill. On her way a wolf wanted her grapes, she wouldn't let him. When she got there, her granny's appearance had changed. 'What big teeth you have!'
'All the better to eat you.'
She ran out terrified.

Sophie Canton (9)
Cadland Primary School, Holbury

Tiny Tales Southern England

Friday

I walked into the building, terrified. I walked down the silent corridor. Shadows in every room. Whispers were heard in big crowded corners. I smelt the air. I was walking down corridor eight. I got closer to room thirteen. It was Friday. That means double maths for this horrible day.

Daisy Price (9)
Cadland Primary School, Holbury

Surprise

The house was in pitch-black! I heard a creak. The lounge door flung open! My tummy rumbled! *'Surprise!'*
It scared the life out of me. We played pass the parcel, it was fun. We had loads of fun playing and dancing. It was the best day of my life.

Chloe Argent (9)
Cadland Primary School, Holbury

Tiny Tales Southern England

The Terror

I was walking up, I was frightened, I got to the top. I was scared, terrified in fact, but my brother pushed me. I fell through a tunnel into a pit of water. I thought I was drowning.
I wish, I wish I wasn't scared of water slides.

Ryan Harris (10)
Cadland Primary School, Holbury

Something!

There was once a something. It looked as if it was black and white. As I watched I started sweating enough to fill the ocean. It had sharp teeth. I turned around and he was gone. I screamed. I fell, he was on me. I was dead! He was full!

Daniel Sharp (10)
Cadland Primary School, Holbury

Fear In My Garden ...

My hands trembled, sweat dribbled down my face, my body was urging me back but I forced myself to do it. I reached out to touch the ferocious, hairy beast, teeth as sharp as knives. 'Argh it's making a strange noise?' I exploded with fear. *Miaow!*

Alisha Carrigan (10)
Cottesmore St Mary's RC School, Hove

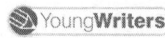

Sea Adventures

There I was on Morooners Island exchanging insults with a pirate, while clanking my sword against his. I stumbled on a stick and found myself lying on the ground with a sword rested against my neck. I grabbed the sword, clutching it tight in my hands.
'Say your last words!'

Hannah Donaghy (10)
Cottesmore St Mary's RC School, Hove

The Story Of Stonehenge

The village storyteller stepped onto the stage. 'I'm going to tell you about Stonehenge,' he said, 'Stonehenge is a copy of Raven's Gate. In the beginning of time, five defeated the greatest evil. They banished it to another dimension. Raven's Gate was the closed link to it.' Then he left.

Bethan Clark (10)
Cottesmore St Mary's RC School, Hove

One Letter In Fifty Words

Ouch, forced into flat space and stamped on.
Pushed into hole, falling down dark tunnel.
Shoved into sack for long journey. Sorted! Plop through hole.
'The post's here!'
Fast fingers roughly tear. At last light! *Scream!*
'I've done it Mum, I'm going to uni.'
Sloppy kisses, pride of place! Worthwhile.

Madeleine Hanford (10)
Harlands Primary School, Uckfield

Stormy Day

One stormy day young Danny was bored because he couldn't go outside, so he decided to play a game of 'play a trick on my sister', so he dressed up as an evil space monkey and crept into the living room. At the sight of her brother she ran away.

George Reed (10)
Harlands Primary School, Uckfield

The Orchestra

Honk went the bassoon as the thunderous orchestra began the long symphony. The noise filled the gigantic church and flew through the church doors. As the beautiful sounds drifted through the air, the poor and lonely villagers paused to listen to the glorious sounds. It stopped. Was it a dream?

Emily Muxworthy (9)
Harlands Primary School, Uckfield

The Familiar Surprise

With intense fear Theo walked the dark, eerie alley. Stormclouds covered the moon. The misty air was heavy with silence. Eyes burnt into his neck. A rasping breath traced his faltering steps. Gathering his courage he turned to face his assailant. There before him stood … his pet cat Wesley!

Kitty Ziolek (10)
Harlands Primary School, Uckfield

The Magic Rainbow

Amy was a young girl. One day it was raining very hard and Amy was looking out of the window to see what was happening. A bright flash sparkled out of nowhere. Amy ran outside and there was a sparkly, shiny rainbow. Then it started to talk …

Anastasia Hiscox (8)
Harlands Primary School, Uckfield

The Spider

There it was. The hairy tickly creature running up my legs. 'Get it off!' I shrieked, but no one heard me. The spider ran up me, oh no, another spider ran up my leg. Two, I can't have two! I'm afraid. They were very hairy, 'Get them off!' I shrieked.

Aoife McManus (9)
Harlands Primary School, Uckfield

Midnight Horror!

As the clock struck twelve the lights went out. The door creaked and the radiator burst and the cat shrieked. The thunder started slowly at first and then *boom!* He was all alone sitting by his bedside. Suddenly something zoomed past his head. He knew something was there but what … ?

Ellie Tew (11)
Harlands Primary School, Uckfield

Woody

He was sat by the door waiting and waiting, all he could see was an empty drive. Half an hour later he was still there waiting and waiting. His owner would be back in an hour but till then he was waiting. At last his owner returned. Finally, teatime.

Lily Wanless (8)
Harlands Primary School, Uckfield

The Show Must Go On

'Daisy, fantastic you've got the lead in the play. You know all your lines? No problem,' calmed Milly.
One week passed and the big day came.
'I've got stage fright,' whispered Daisy. She couldn't go on, who could save the day? 'Milly, you know all my lines, please.'
'Here goes!'

Darcy Brown (7)
Harlands Primary School, Uckfield

The Boy Who Got Scared

One day Harry was watching TV, his brother came in the room and kept making scary noises. Harry thought it was the TV, was it? He didn't know so he hid behind the sofa. As he was going to hide behind the sofa, his brother jumped and scared him.

Robert Miller (10)
Harlands Primary School, Uckfield

The Monster's Fist

Once a long, long time ago a huge, two-metre-tall monster with ten tonne fists started killing everybody in town. With one swipe of a ten tonne fist people's heads split!
The people dug down into the heart and split it in half! And the monster died almost immediately.

Charlie Tatnall (9)
Harlands Primary School, Uckfield

The Audition

I was standing outside sweating madly, waiting. Finally I got taken inside, standing there before the judges I opened my mouth but nothing came out. I was too nervous to sing. I ran, I would never become famous if I was too scared to even audition for a school play!

Sarah Romilly (11)
Highfield CE Primary School, Southampton

The Hungry Beast

There it stood before me, waiting for its prey to go by. Luckily it was in its cage; circling round in it. Suddenly it caught its feast, wriggling round in its talons. Then in a flash its cage opened, its door squeaking.
'Mum, the budgie's flown away!'
'Then catch it!'

Ivan Zheludev (11)
Highfield CE Primary School, Southampton

Tranquil

I glided down to the big blue bottom, iridescent sapphire bubbles emerging and rippling around, the buoyant aqua encircling me. I waved my arms around the turquoise paradise, yet instead of moving myself along, I hit a hard object; but it was only my sister. I arose, began to laugh.

Cleome Rawnsley (10)
Highfield CE Primary School, Southampton

That's Not My Reflection

I poured the bubbly, slimy liquid into the container. Metallic purple and black swirled around and settled to a deep mysterious colour. *This is it,* I thought, holding up the container proudly and taking a sip. Suddenly I felt my body stretching - what's happening? I saw my reflection … and screamed.

Tina Wu (11)
Highfield CE Primary School, Southampton

The Watch From Outer Space

Suddenly Tom heard a crash and ran to see what it was. The pod opened, it was a watch from outer space! Then Tom put it on, there was a green flash then a screech. We could turn into aliens whenever we wanted!
'Wow wait till I tell Mum.'

Zenobia Summers (11)
Highfield CE Primary School, Southampton

Potion Darkness

He slowly paced over to the cauldron, not spilling anything from the mixture. The thick, sloppy, vivid, orange mixture glowed, bubbling away in the container. Somehow it knew what was going to happen and it really liked it! Dr Vandel poured the sloppy mixture. Suddenly a mythical monster appeared.

Joseph D'Souza (11)
Highfield CE Primary School, Southampton

Untitled

Pink Bunny was having a picnic when all of a sudden, creeping through the bushes came Wolf. 'I'm hungry.' His mouth watered at the sight of Bunny. Then he pounced.
Pink Bunny jumped up, 'I do karate,' Bunny screamed, Bunny kicked Wolf, Wolf ran away, never to be seen again.

Natalie Ertl (11)
Highfield CE Primary School, Southampton

Death House

Hey, where am I? Bob looked around the creepy broken house. Rain shot down on Bob like bullets. The rats scurried around the damp floor. Bob crept around a corner. Suddenly a huge creature smashed through the wall and screeched. It grabbed Bob, Bob screamed only to await his doom.

Ramzan Bilal (11)
Highfield CE Primary School, Southampton

Penguin Chase

Once there was a penguin that was in serious danger. A leopard seal was chasing him. Leopard seals are very vicious and fast. The penguin had no chance. Suddenly Reubeno the pengueno came to the rescue. Reubeno, the pengueno, picked up a rock and threw it. The predator swam away.

Reuben Vulliamy (11)
Highfield CE Primary School, Southampton

Mars-Epan

I jumped into my spaceship and took off for Mars! At last we landed, I had a good walk round and found a country called Mars-Epan! Mars bars roamed the country. I said hello to everyone and then shot off in my spaceship. The journey had ended, or had it … ?

Christie Arnold (11)
Highfield CE Primary School, Southampton

The Horror Needle

Eyes narrowing, hands twitching with sweat dripping from head to toe. I sat on a bed. Then a figure appeared in front of me and said, 'This won't hurt a bit!' Then a needle jabbed deep into my arm and before I knew it I was out the doctor's surgery.

Jasmeet Khalsa (11)
Highfield CE Primary School, Southampton

The Big Kayak Race

Bill was in a kayak race, he got into his wetsuit and into his kayak and got a paddle. But if he fell out then he was out. Bill fell out almost at the finish line. But he was stuck! Would he get out or would he drown?

Freddie Chart (11)
Highfield CE Primary School, Southampton

Tiny Tales Southern England

The Field Demon

Jack the foolish jackdaw was rooting around the crop fields searching for seeds. Suddenly, he looked up. What he saw scared the life out of him. There was one of those humans! This one was in wellies; and loose straw stuck to his old overcoat. Jack fainted. The scarecrow smiled.

Hugo Wolfe (11)
Highfield CE Primary School, Southampton

Old Friend

'Who are you?' screamed Lucy, terrified.
'Don't you remember your old friend?'
'No,' said Lucy.
'Well, you threw me in the toilet!' screamed the teddy.
Then the teddy stabbed Lucy in her leg.
His face smiled. He was dreaming of such fascinating revenge. She was bleeding hard but luckily survived.

Matt Mors (11)
Highfield CE Primary School, Southampton

Tiny Tales Southern England

Muddle Up Mary

Once there was a wicked witch called Mary whose evil spells kept going wrong. She wanted to be ugly but made herself beautiful. Her pet frog got turned into a butterfly instead of a bat. Her friend Milly laughed at her. Mary tried to make Milly disappear but disappeared herself!

Summer Brighton (8)
Icklesham CE Primary School, Icklesham

The Journey

I pulled up my duvet and snuggled up and slipped into a dream … as I awoke I found myself on a unicorn's back. I saw I was holding silken diamond ribbons.
As I was falling asleep I found myself back in bed but holding gold and silver strands of mane.

Georgia Dalley (8)
Kings Copse Primary School, Southampton

Tiny Tales Southern England

Sports Day

I started to run like I never had before, I was far ahead; but then I tripped and went flying forward and sprained my ankle, although, I got up and started to limp as fast as I could. And then all of a sudden I stopped … I'd *won* the race!

Nick Roberts (10)
Kings Copse Primary School, Southampton

Here It Comes!

I am behind the sofa waiting, *pitter-patter*, here it comes. I hope it won't come to me. *Pitter-patter!* It is getting closer! *Squeak!* Light beams in. I can see a shadow. It's coming closer, closer and closer. Suddenly, *pounce!* He has found me. Here is my pet dog!

Dylan Thorpe (10)
Kings Copse Primary School, Southampton

Tiny Tales Southern England

The Day I Met An Alien!

I looked at it. It was an alien. It looked back. I didn't speak, but suddenly, it spoke. I was scared and I didn't know what to do. I had to talk, so I did. It smiled. I thought I was fine, but when it opened its mouth, I wasn't …

Emma Green (10)
Kings Copse Primary School, Southampton

Aliens Dread Roller Coasters!

In my land, a new invention came! One that dreaded every second in my life. I couldn't help it! I was too afraid. Although I was being silly; I couldn't control it! Thinking about loops, going upside down and, oh the screams. Absolutely horrible!

The moment came – dreaded roller coaster …

Holly (10)
Kings Copse Primary School, Southampton

The Chessington Horror

I was so anxious to go to Chessington. Then as I walked upstairs to a ride; I trembled! My heart was beating so hard and speedily, it felt like ten thousand drumsticks were pounding on a substantial drum at the same time … ! My friends encouraged me to go on rides.

Sommer Ledger (9)
Kings Copse Primary School, Southampton

The Monstrous Aliens

On planet Earth, there was … Uncle Earl! Uncle Earl created weird things for 'science experiments'. It was just a normal boring day (as usual). Suddenly a whizzing whirlpool appeared out of nowhere! Uncle Earl just stood there, he was gobsmacked.
With his heart beating, he shouted, 'The aliens are back!'

Ailish Setford (10)
Kings Copse Primary School, Southampton

Electric Doors

I trembled and shook, with butterflies in my tummy. I was so shaky; I almost fainted with my knees knocking hard. But I slowly and bravely stepped forward. Well, unfortunately, I hesitated but I stood strongly and went through so quickly.
I do wish I wasn't afraid of electric doors!

Alex Dallimore (10)
Kings Copse Primary School, Southampton

Ghost In The House

One day Emily went home from school. But when she got home ... there was no one there, she was scared. Then a ghost grabbed her. She screamed, 'Argh!' He took her to his lair. Suddenly she woke up and realised it was just a dream. She was so, so happy.

Megan Williams (10)
Kings Copse Primary School, Southampton

The Cursed Apple

Snow White bit into a bright red apple. A few seconds later her face turned red, to orange, to green and she fell *thump!* on the floor!
Eight minutes later Prince Charming tried to help her. 'Will you let me go!' she shouted, 'I'm having a lie down!'

Charlotte Lewis
Kings Copse Primary School, Southampton

The Monster In The House

The terrifying shape of the monster moved slowly across the wall coming closer. I hid in the monster's lair. I could hear his footsteps coming, 'Argh!' I screamed. Its footsteps stopped, I could only hear him crying. *Phew,* I'm glad my brother Sam has gone!

Peter Kidd (8)
Kings Copse Primary School, Southampton

Tiny Tales Southern England

Katie, William And The Wicked Witch

Once a girl called Katie lived in a castle. She had three godmothers, one blue, one green, one pink.
One morning Katie picked blackberries. The godmothers were making cake with a prince called William. The evil witch took William away, but Katie saved him. They got married.

Lauren Merritt (8)
Kings Copse Primary School, Southampton

The Spooky Light

One night Sam was in bed, there was a sudden flash of light, suddenly the door opened, the light came into Sam's bedroom. Sam hid under his cover.
'Sam, it's only me, the lights have gone out.'

William Churcher (8)
Kings Copse Primary School, Southampton

The Spooky Monster

I peeked out of my covers and turned right to left. Suddenly I heard something bang, it sounded like someone stamping up the stairs. The door creaked open. My face turned white. I shook like an ice cube, but it was only my mum.

Sherrie Hall (8)
Kings Copse Primary School, Southampton

The Creepy Shadow

The creepy shadow moved swiftly across the wall. It came closer and closer and reached out to grab me. I quickly turned on the light, 'Mum,' I said,' you have a very scary shadow.'
'So you thought I was a monster?'
'Yes Mum I did.'

Samantha Marsh (7)
Kings Copse Primary School, Southampton

The Fall

Ella tried to climb up the large, tall mountain. Her face went bright pink as she started to lose her grip. She thought she was going to fall. Just then she lost her grip and down she came. *Weee,* she whizzed down the slide and landed with an immense thud.

Emily Sprenger (7)
Kings Copse Primary School, Southampton

The Surprise

I got back from school, the hall was dark and all the room lights were flickering. But one room was not, one at the end of the hall. I could hear creaking and scratching, I turned the light on, 'Surprise! Happy birthday Chloe!'
'Thanks, I'm so glad!'

Carys Cotton (8)
Kings Copse Primary School, Southampton

Tiny Tales Southern England

Something

He sat behind the sofa. Something was after him but he wouldn't let it get him. He peeked round the sofa. The door creaked open. He saw something. It came closer and closer. 'Argh!' he cried.
'What's wrong my dear?' asked Mum.

Joseph Harding (8)
Kings Copse Primary School, Southampton

My Birthday

My smile is like a banana over my mouth. I creep downstairs into the living room. 'Surprise!' Mum is there and she is holding a huge cake. In my excitement I run up to the cake without seeing the ribbons on the floor, *splat!* I fall in the cake.

Rory Clarke (9)
Kings Copse Primary School, Southampton

Tiny Tales Southern England

Spiro The Dragon

One afternoon Grendor got so mad and froze all the fairies one by one. Grendor's dad told Spiro and he set off. Soon Spiro came to Sparke's house. He asked if she could come and help him and so they both set off. Grendor got madder and froze them both.

Celest Dring (9)
Kings Copse Primary School, Southampton

Miaows In The Night

I lie in bed, when suddenly I hear a noise. I clamber out of bed. My heart pounds as I open the door. I suddenly feel fur pressing against my legs. I hear a hungry *miaow*, flick on the light and see Emily pawing at her bowl!

George Wright (9)
Kings Copse Primary School, Southampton

The Magical Dream

I snuggle up in my cuddly duvet. Suddenly I feel myself flying swiftly through the air on a magic unicorn, holding on to its soft, silken, golden mane. The night sadly ends but as I awake from the magic dream I find I am holding some soft, silken, golden mane.

Katie Dalmas (9)
Kings Copse Primary School, Southampton

The Big Race

Here I am at the big race, when the ref says, 'Go.' *Vroom!* Off we go. *Whee!* A 360° turn *erggg!* Here comes the roundabout, *argh!* Gosh this is fabulous for a go-kart.
For a minute then I thought I was Michael Schumacher.

Elliott Prince (9)
Kings Copse Primary School, Southampton

The Hairy Monster

Tom was in the kitchen, all alone. He suddenly heard the door creaking. 'Where's my mum?' he cried. He was sure the hairy monster was waiting for him.
The door opened. He got his spoonful of cereal ready to get him. *Splat!* It was Mum.
'Sorry!' he cried shakily.

Thomas Edwards (9)
Kings Copse Primary School, Southampton

The Magical Flight

Katie was going shopping. She suddenly felt herself lifting into the air, she was suddenly flying. She was now whizzing around Tesco and everything she wanted was floating ready for her. Her mouth dropped. She landed at home and all of the shopping was unpacked. Katie was absolutely breathless, 'Phew!'

George Gough (9)
Kings Copse Primary School, Southampton

A Bizarre Journey

Geoff was thirsty, he drank some milk. He drifted off to sleep. After a while he awoke. Everything was made of chocolate, it was fabulous. His eyes were glimmering with joy. Geoff felt a nudge on his shoulder, 'Wake up Geoff it's bedtime.'
It was a dream!

Jeff Damerell (9)
Kings Copse Primary School, Southampton

The Monster

I looked on the floor. I looked outside the tent. The monster was nowhere to be seen. I turned off my light and snuggled into my sleeping bag. Suddenly I felt eight hairy legs crawl up my leg. I jumped out of my sleeping bag.
Argh!' I screamed, 'a spider!'

Annabelle Ede (8)
Kings Copse Primary School, Southampton

Creepy

I walk into this place with cobwebs on the wall. I see a skeleton on the floor, I feel something touch me. *Argh!* Lightning strikes down in that scary way. I see pumpkins on the floor.
'Are you OK dear? It's Hallowe'en you know,' said Mum.

Nathaniel O'Horan (9)
Kings Copse Primary School, Southampton

Down On The Farm

One day a boy went down to the farm, cows mooed, ducks quacked, horses nodded at him. He met a Billy goat. He suddenly got scared to walk past it! His family got past perfectly all right! So he shuffled past it very slowly and looked at the other animals.

Charlie Conlon (10)
Kings Copse Primary School, Southampton

Spelling Test!

It's so silent I can hear my own heart beating. I feel butterflies in my tummy. Oh why am I here once again? Every week I say I'm not going to but here I am, waiting. I take a big puff, I can't get out of it!
'Spelling time children!'

Katy Conlon (8)
Kings Copse Primary School, Southampton

A Holiday Of A Lifetime

There once was a family. One day their huge cream camel went missing when they were on holiday. They had a long treacherous journey travelling round the world looking for it, 'Oh no! Mum, I've found it! I had forgotten I'd tied it to the caravan.'

'Silly boy,' sighed Mum.

Jonathan Guy (9)
Kings Copse Primary School, Southampton

The Ghost In Top Hat And Tails

Mum screamed, 'Ghost! It's wearing top hat and tails!' Running into her bedroom I switched on the light, she was screaming, 'Ghost!' Laughing I said, 'Look Mum it's the way Dad's jacket's hanging on your wardrobe and your hat's on top, it's your mind playing tricks.' We both laughed.

Alex Papanicolaou (8)
Our Lady of Lourdes RC Primary School, Rottingdean

The Vampire's Haunt

There used to be a vampire that haunted the city every night. The vampire's name was Martin, he dressed up every night to haunt the city.

One night someone cut his costume apart and they saw it was a boy on stilts. He fell off his stilts and became good.

George Turner (8)
Our Lady of Lourdes RC Primary School, Rottingdean

What A Call

I woke up with a call from the phone. I got up and answered it. A lady said I'd won one million pounds but I didn't believe her because I'd had calls from competitions that don't exist, but then I remembered that I'd entered one last week.
What a call.

Grace Walker (9)
Our Lady of Lourdes RC Primary School, Rottingdean

The Racing Car

David and George were on a race team. David wasn't very happy that George always got the fastest car, so David poured sugar into the tank of George's car so he would win.
The next day their manager said, 'David, you can have the faster car today.' And George won!

Jack Dunsmore (9)
Our Lady of Lourdes RC Primary School, Rottingdean

The Seed

I was planted deep into the ground, where worms slimed around the mud and chalky stones. All that I had to eat was myself. It was a race for life. I passed through clumps of mud and little pieces of wood. Finally I made it out into the open world.

Thomas Greenstein (10)
Our Lady of Lourdes RC Primary School, Rottingdean

No One

I thought someone was following me. I looked round. No one was there. I carried on walking, I felt a hand on my shoulder, again, no one was there. I saw my front door. The doorknob was a sinister face. Inside, I looked in the mirror. No one was there …

Juliet Maxted (9)
Our Lady of Lourdes RC Primary School, Rottingdean

Tiny Tales Southern England

My Evening Fright

I was in bed when I heard the door creak open. Then a sinister sound carried itself nearer and nearer. Two metallic green eyes were staring at me. I pulled my sheet up to my chin and closed my eyes. Then it hit me.
'Argh,' I said, 'get off Puss!'

Alex Maxted (9)
Our Lady of Lourdes RC Primary School, Rottingdean

A Magic Spell That Goes Wrong

Emma concocted a spell for her grandma who was ill. She added the purple powder to make you lively then the green powder to make you feel joyful. Suddenly she realised that she had added the ingredients the wrong way round. 'Oh no!' gasped Emma as Grandma turned into a …

Kezia Quarrie-Jones (8)
St Alban's CE(A) Primary School, Havant

Tiny Tales Southern England

The Bad Trip

I sat down, something was clutching my stomach. It was swirling and going up and down and up and down. I could not handle it anymore! I opened my eyes, I realised I wasn't tied up, I was just making a big fuss because I was car sick. *Blearhh!*

Imogen Walsh (8)
St Alban's CE(A) Primary School, Havant

I'm Just Crackers About Cheese!

Wallace and Gromit ran out of cheese. They both knew the moon was made out of cheese. So they got their crackers and zoomed off in their shiny rocket. On arrival they gouged a huge hole and that is why you see a crescent moon in the sky.

Emily Frost (8)
St Alban's CE(A) Primary School, Havant

Tiny Tales Southern England

Loch Ness Triangle

The final race is about to begin. Lock Ness vs K9. Loch Ness goes zooming before K9 can even start! Loch Ness doesn't see he goes into the Bermuda Triangle. He is trapped in a cage! Loch Ness gets out! He's back in the real world and wins the race!

Alice Kaminski (8)
St Alban's CE(A) Primary School, Havant

It('s)

It was fine, I thought to myself, my heart about to explode. I took a step nearer, wiping sweat from my forehead. Its long string body lay stretched out along with its slimy skin covering its companions.
I really wish I did not have such a fear of spaghetti!

Joanne Marshall
St Alban's CE(A) Primary School, Havant

Mr Bean's Gymnastics Experience

Mr Bean decided to try a gymnastics class. He was very nervous! The teacher was plump and the students looked very competent. Mr Bean attempted the parallel bars, flew through the air and fell. His toes ended up in his ears and he could not prise them out!

Georgina Mellor (9)
St Alban's CE(A) Primary School, Havant

The Scary Monster

My hands trembled and sweat crept down the back of my spine as the shadowy creature entered my line of vision. Beady eyes glared into mine. Razor-sharp claws scraped the floor. The snake-like tail sliced through the air. I don't know why I'm so scared of my gerbil!

Katie Gould (10)
St Alban's CE(A) Primary School, Havant

Tiny Tales Southern England

A Dangerous Mission

We had finally arrived! We took a deep breath and cautiously sneaked into Tesco. The savage natives were snatching all they could find. Mum peered through the veg as I dashed to get the milk. At the checkout our adventure was over! 'Same time next week?' said Mum.

Madeleine Spice (9)
St Alban's CE(A) Primary School, Havant

The Mistake

The gerbil came snuffling out of its hole. A monster stood before it. The cat swiped with its razor-sharp claws! Whack! The cat stood twitching! 'Oh no Co-Co, have you smacked the gerbil house again? I told you it's not a forcefield! It is a glass tank!'

Nicholas Robertson (9)
St Alban's CE(A) Primary School, Havant

Home Alone

Home alone, every kid's dream. Not mine! Being home alone makes me scared stiff. Suddenly, the noise of banging on the door assaults my ears. I daren't open the door. A roar! I run upstairs, petrified by the roaring I peer out of the window. It's my best friend!

Daniel Mann (10)
St Alban's CE(A) Primary School, Havant

The Race

I approached the starting line and took a deep breath. I heard a sound and saw everyone run. My legs felt weak, but I couldn't fail. I jogged, but gradually got faster. Soon I was running with still a mile to go. I finished the race and came … *last!*

Mollie Griffiths (9)
St Alban's CE(A) Primary School, Havant

Nearly Dead

I started to feel sick, my head was banging. Dad looked unconscious with blood on his face, or was it? I turned away not wanting to look. Something moved behind me. Dad was sitting up licking blood, (or was it) off his face.
'Tasty ketchup this is,' he said.
'Daaad!'

Johanna Horsman (9)
St Alban's CE(A) Primary School, Havant

The Shopping Trip

I was out shopping with my friend when we suddenly found ourselves being chased. Finally we reached my cottage, Red Riding Hood, breathless, gasped, 'Snow White, I get chased by the wolf!'

'That's funny! I get chased by the witch all the time!' I replied.

Amy Frost (9)
St Alban's CE(A) Primary School, Havant

Tiny Tales Southern England

Mr Bean Gets Married

Crash, Mr Bean threw teddy onto the floor. *Tooot!* Taxi here, off he went thinking he'd forgotten something. Eventually his fiancée trotted down the aisle.
'You may kiss the bride.'
She lifted her veil. Mr Bean ran in the opposite direction, screaming. He'd forgotten to check her face!

Matthew Lee (9)
St Alban's CE(A) Primary School, Havant

The Monkey

Mum, Eddy and Dad arrive at Tesco. Dad went away to the clothes department leaving Eddy behind with an annoyed mum.

A few minutes later a monkey leapt down the aisle. Eddy climbed on the monkey. The monkey cried, 'Get off!'

The monkey was Eddy's dad in a new costume.

Euan Langford
St Alban's CE(A) Primary School, Havant

Ahh The Merry-Go-Round

Sweat slowly tickled.
'My throat,' I whined and kicked, I didn't want to go but my parents forced me. Tears poured from my face. My body was aching badly, it felt like I wanted to faint. My brain hurt. Time to go on the merry-go-round.

Georgina Mason (8)
St Alban's CE(A) Primary School, Havant

The Famous Unicorn Disappears

In the kingdom of Fraziza lived a unicorn. This unicorn flew like the birds but one day she decided to explore the Atlantic Ocean. After planning she was soon soaring in the air. Suddenly … she dropped into the mists of time. The legend of the train was true.

Chloe Anderson (8)
St Alban's CE(A) Primary School, Havant

Magical Forest

One dark gloomy night a young girl wandered into a forest to spot deer. Suddenly out of the dark shadow stood a glimmering white unicorn. She snatched her phone for help, accidentally taking a photo. In the blink of an eye the phone and unicorn turned to ash, she screamed …

Daniel Aspey (9)
St Alban's CE(A) Primary School, Havant

Guarding Dog

I was walking my dog along the street when out of nowhere a tall grizzly bear stood before me. My brave dog ran up and bit him hard! Then a man pulled the suit off holding his bleeding leg!

Liam Thomas (10)
St Alban's CE(A) Primary School, Havant

Goodbye Cruel World

Jay was an ugly man who'd never had a girlfriend. Everybody who saw him ran.
One day he looked in the mirror and realised why, pimples! He decided to go to the roof of his tower block.
'Goodbye cruel world!' and he applied the acne cream …
He married in September.

Joseph Walsh (9)
St Alban's CE(A) Primary School, Havant

It

There he is sharpening his blade-like teeth with a lump of wood. His bristly fur sticking out like thorns, the eyes he has are big, his excellent hearing can detect the smallest of sounds, I tread towards him and pick up my little hamster.

Hannah Aspley (10)
St Alban's CE(A) Primary School, Havant

Lighting The Fuse

He lit the fuse. I stood well back awaiting the loud noise. A crackle could be heard. *When would it go off?* I thought. My house could be shattered by the force. Suddenly it exploded. Sparks flew through the air. The colours faded. I was ready for another firework.

Amy Shepherd (9)
St Alban's CE(A) Primary School, Havant

The Needle

I dropped into the plastic seat, petrified. 'Alicia please.' I tried to make my feet walk into the blue room with little success. However, I managed to fall onto the clinical bed. The needle was huge.
'This won't hurt sweetie.' *Prick.*
I wish I wasn't so scared of injections!

Alicia Carpenter (10)
St Alban's CE(A) Primary School, Havant

Tiny Tales Southern England

The World Of Dinosaurs

One day at a zoo a lady called Abby was just feeding some iguanas when … they all hid.
Tick, tick, tick.
'Boss,' she shouted to scare the iguanas. 'Turn the clocks off please.'
'Wait!' he shouted from his office. Then she saw … *blood!*

Alfie Simms (8)
St Alban's CE(A) Primary School, Havant

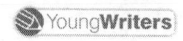

Horror In The House!

Helen walked into her house and heard screaming behind the door … Helen yanked open the door and saw a vampire attacking her mum! Helen leapt out to save her mum from the vampire …

'Cut!' A film maker opened the door. So it was a film clip after all!

Holly Horn (8)
St Alban's CE(A) Primary School, Havant

The Evil Experiment

Finally the time had come, the cute little experiment was completed. Its wide puppy-dog eyes and sweet fluffy face covered up the true power of this deceiving little beast. The mad professor had no idea of the damage this deadly creature could unleash on its unlucky prey …

Laurie Harman (11)
St Joseph's RC Primary School, Christchurch

The Mona

Mona was a massive sea monster. One day it crushed a gigantic ship called the Titanic. The Titanic started sinking. The people panicked and jumped off the ship. It was now at the bottom of the sea! Mona was now a big threat to the people on the ship!

Pierre Cochart (10)
St Joseph's RC Primary School, Christchurch

The Black Phoenix

As I was climbing the spectacular Atlantic mountain, it shot out a massive black phoenix covered in golden lightning stripes. He had fiery eyes and icy wings that looked like they had been carved by God. His power was yet to be unleashed. I blinked and he was gone!

Reuben King (11)
St Joseph's RC Primary School, Christchurch

Evil Trevor

It was green, bubbly and dreadful. The potion was sure to kill anyone who drank it. So, that was what evil Trevor was going to plant in the royal family's tea. This was sure to kill them. Then evil Trevor would next be king! His plan would never fail!

Jack Myers (11)
St Joseph's RC Primary School, Christchurch

Tiny Tales Southern England

Lost In Time!

They began to curiously walk through the woods. Step by step rustling the leaves beneath their shivering feet. They ran on. To their excitement they found a rusty box. Both of them stepped into it. They felt extremely dizzy. In a matter of 10 seconds they were lost in time!

Seana Morrison (11)
St Joseph's RC Primary School, Christchurch

Help!

Where am I? I awoke in a dark, deserted room. It was only me, I was petrified. There was a figure, a dark mysterious figure tucked up tight in the corner. I heard a rustle. *'Rats!'* I screamed. I eagerly sprinted to the door! It was locked! There's no escape!

Natalie Dunn (11)
St Joseph's RC Primary School, Christchurch

The Dragon

Billy walked slowly towards the room. He swung the door open to find a dark desolate room with a dark figure on the wall. He was looking closely to find out what the figure was. It was a fierce, mean dragon. *'Argh!'* he screamed. Flames burst out. Suddenly Billy disappeared.

Amelia Butt (11)
St Joseph's RC Primary School, Christchurch

The Boy That Was Not To Be Seen

Sam was cycling speedily home, when he saw something mysterious staring in the distance. Sam stood silent gazing at this ancient house. He walked in slowly through the door, as it creaked open. A bullet was shot. It flew like lightning. Sam was never to be seen again!

Molly Board (11)
St Joseph's RC Primary School, Christchurch

Tiny Tales Southern England

Untitled

Mark pushed open the door and walked straight through thinking nothing was in there, however there were spiders and rats and he was petrified of them. He shouted, 'Help!' Nobody answered. He ran as fast as he could but a monster jumped out at Mark and stabbed him.

Daniel Churchill (11)
St Joseph's RC Primary School, Christchurch

The Greedy Prince

Merlin made a potion to make the prince attractive to the princess because she thought he was greedy. Merlin took the potion and checked it, but suddenly the prince snatched it and drank it, just before Merlin could tell him it was a frog potion! The prince became a frog!

Bradley Ford (11)
St Joseph's RC Primary School, Christchurch

Tiny Tales Southern England

Ginger Breaks Free

Tilly and her horse Ginger lived on a farm in the countryside, until one day Ginger broke out of her field into the forest.
Five minutes later, Ginger knew she was alone. Ginger saw a hunter and galloped. Then she was on the trail home and she smelt fresh oats.

Sophie Livsey (11)
St Joseph's RC Primary School, Christchurch

The Deadly Disappearance

As the lonely leprechaun travelled through the village, he found a large hole, so he climbed into it and heard screeching and squeaking noises and with a blink of an eye, he disappeared.
Nobody has seen him since. All the cops found was a puddle of slimy, blue, runny blood.

James Wheeler (10)
St Joseph's RC Primary School, Christchurch

The Disappearing Girl

The sun was shining while Rebecca was skipping through the rustling trees. She bumped into a huge man. He held out a tiny bottle. Rebecca slowly snatched it and sprinted home in fear.

She laid it on her bed and sat down. The potion fell. Rebecca disappeared!

Anna Davies (10)
St Joseph's RC Primary School, Christchurch

Away Out At Sea

I was lost away out at sea. Nothing more than myself as company. I saw a bright beam of light on the horizon. I felt a strange sensation and went all dizzy. What happened? What could it be? I suddenly vanished, never to be seen again!

Elysha Riordan (11)
St Joseph's RC Primary School, Christchurch

The Lost Girl

The wind was howling through her ears. She could see the light from the lighthouse gleaming through the darkness. She had to reach it. It was her only hope of safety. *'Argh!'* screamed Sarah. She had fallen into the dark icy lake, never to be seen or heard again.

Alice Marshall (11)
St Joseph's RC Primary School, Christchurch

The Mysterious Castle

The trees, which were gnarled and twisted, surrounded the forbidden, dark forest. Sophie's heart trembled as she followed the stony path, which lead to the mysterious castle. Finally she reached the almighty door. Sophie opened the creaking door and all of a sudden she disappeared in a cloud of smoke.

Soniya Santhosh (11)
St Joseph's RC Primary School, Christchurch

Tiny Tales Southern England

The Scream

Sally swung open the door, 'Mum?' She should be home by now.
Suddenly there was a scream from upstairs. She clutched her bag. Sally swerved up the wooden staircase. She tiptoed into her bedroom. Sally's mum was lying on the floor, white. Sally snatched the phone. The line was dead!

Bethany Tyler (11)
St Joseph's RC Primary School, Christchurch

The Evil Bird

A cool bird of prey was casually flying when he accidentally flew into a window. Inside the window was a rat and he swooped down to grab it. He did and then he found some other birds and tried to eat them. He wanted to be the head bird forever.

Jacob Knight (10)
St Joseph's RC Primary School, Christchurch

Tiny Tales Southern England

Alien

A fluorescent light gleamed in the sky. The ray forced Peter to the ground, as it got closer. Then a beam started to lift him towards the light. He reached some sort of plane.
Suddenly someone started saying, 'Become one of us!'
Then *boom!* A different Peter. An alien Peter!

Thomas Finch (11)
St Joseph's RC Primary School, Christchurch

Surprise

It was a dark night; Lola and Bonny were on their way home. They walked through the dark forest, they were cold and frightened.
Finally they arrived home but no one was there. The house was bare on Lola's special night, then suddenly they heard something.
'Surprise!' shouted their parents.

Lois Bell (10)
St Jude's RC Primary School, Fareham

Tiny Tales Southern England

Moving Away

It was a lovely day at school, Lottie and Maisy were playing outside, when Kerrie came and told them some news. She was to move to Australia. Her friends were shocked. Kerrie said her dad got a new job there so they'd have to move, 'But I don't want to!'

Molly Hamilton (10)
St Jude's RC Primary School, Fareham

Bombed!

We were going to the shelter near the park. I could see them coming towards London. I could hear them too. Flames flickering, houses blowing up. They're coming and I'm really scared. Why here and not somewhere else? I know they've bombed our house. I wish the war wasn't now!

Lauren Brown (10)
St Jude's RC Primary School, Fareham

A Spell That Went Wrong

The witch was testing a new spell. She was trying to take over the world. The evil witch was making this poison with two dogs' eyeballs and the blood of a crocodile. When the last drop of blood was put into the bottle, it exploded and killed the witch.

Cameron Smith (10)
St Jude's RC Primary School, Fareham

The Wrong Spell

The black cauldron was overflowing with green bubbly liquid. The smell was unbearable, as the witch had put all different types of ingredients in. Suddenly, the witch knew that she had the spell completely wrong!

'Mum, the cake's gone wrong!'

Martha North (10)
St Jude's RC Primary School, Fareham

Power Cut

Riley was alone in her room when a sudden power cut struck. *What's that? There's a light coming from under the door.* Riley shivered. The door handle screeched as it opened, 'Riley, I have a lit candle for you.' Riley prayed, said goodnight, blew out the candle and fell asleep.

Grace Baggott (10)
St Jude's RC Primary School, Fareham

A Camping Scare

They were in the woods. Alison and Susan were asleep in their tent. Suddenly something awoke them. Trembling the girls looked in the bushes. Their dad jumped out. 'You scared us,' they said.
'Sorry, I was just checking on you.'
'Argh!'
'Oh no.'

Caroline Duff (10)
St Jude's RC Primary School, Fareham

Home Alone

It was dark, I was in the living room sitting on the sofa, I heard a rumbling noise from the kitchen, I tiptoed up to the door, I was too scared to open it so I waited, then I opened it but it was only the washing machine.

Adam Deary (10)
St Jude's RC Primary School, Fareham

Doom

One day a vicious monster called Grace attacked Rhodes. But a hero was there to save them. He drew his sword and chopped her ear off and stabbed her in the heart. Screeches came out.
He had saved the day once again and everyone was happy.

Stuart Nixon (9)
St Jude's RC Primary School, Fareham

Lost

'Dad I'm going out to play,' said Lucy.
'So are we,' said Arron and Lennon.
'I know,' said Lennon, 'I'm going to play in the haunted house.'
'OK,' said Lucy, 'let's go then.'
'I'm going in,' shouted Lennon.
'Lennon where are you?' said Lucy.
'I'm in the bathroom,' shouted Lennon.

Oliver Pegrum (10)
St Jude's RC Primary School, Fareham

The Surprise Pet

Emma's mum was going to the pet shop to get a rabbit for her daughter. When Emma got home her mum said, 'I've got a surprise for you.'
Emma said, 'Thank you Mum, I am going to call my rabbit Snowy.'
Emma and Snowy lived happily ever after.

Liam Perella (10)
St Jude's RC Primary School, Fareham

The Haunted House

It was a cold, dark night, Paul and John went to the house. When they got to the house Paul knocked on the door but there was no answer, so John pushed the door and they went in the house then a ghost came up to them and said,
'Boo!'

Christopher Lowman (10)
St Jude's RC Primary School, Fareham

Snow White

Snow White's wicked mother had imprisoned her father in a mirror in the centre of the castle! What was she to do? With the help of her seven friends she defeated her mother and saved her father and they all lived happily ever after, except for her wicked mother.

Jodie Harrison (10)
Southway Junior School, Burgess Hill

Tiny Tales

There was once a little girl who loved mermaids. One day she went to the beach with her sister and her mum. She went for a swim. Suddenly she got caught. Something put something on her leg and she grew a tail. What was going to happen?

Satya Ramkissun (9)
Southway Junior School, Burgess Hill

Untitled

I was alone on Hallowe'en. Someone knocked on the door. It gave me a humungous fright, seeing someone in a monster costume. It really looked real. I wasn't quite convinced it was a real human. Suddenly it pulled me away to an old, forgotten prison. It locked me up, *heeelllppp!*

Ellen Shaw (9)
Southway Junior School, Burgess Hill

The Worst Ride Of My Life

My hands were shaking, my lips were trembling, I was holding on so tight but then it happened, we started to go up. I was so scared, where was I? I didn't know what to do. My legs were clanking together, I never realised how bad an escalator ride is.

Amie Tidd (9)
Southway Junior School, Burgess Hill

The Lost Alien

Once in a galaxy far away there was an alien floating through space. He had lost his way home - a nearby spacecraft helped him onboard. He was from the planet Zogg, the crew knew where he lived and they took him home, that was just luck. What happens next …?

Joshua Brown (9)
Southway Junior School, Burgess Hill

The Little Hedgehog

Once upon a time there was a little hedgehog, he sat on a wall to watch the sunset. He saw his favourite food walk past; ants on worms, he tried to get them but slipped and hurt his back, the ants and worms went to see if he was OK.

Eithan-James Smith (8)
Southway Junior School, Burgess Hill

The Spell

'You hurt me, now I will turn you into a frog.' But when Jasmine tried Louise turned into a worm so Jasmine tried again. She kept trying until there was no more magic left in her so Louise was stuck as a snail, but eventually the spell wore off.

Phoebe Turner (10)
Southway Junior School, Burgess Hill

The Mad Scientist

Courtney was down in her science lab mixing up a potion. It was green, gooey and smelt horrid. When she was done she drank the long hair potion to check if it would make her hair grow but it didn't. It made her bald for the rest of her life!

Miranda Hart (9)
Southway Junior School, Burgess Hill

Untitled

A man called Super Sausage saw something in the water and he went to investigate. He was scared. He jumped in and tried to save it. It was not human, he shot it with his meat vision. He tried and tried to kill it but it wasn't working.

Alex Faria (10)
Southway Junior School, Burgess Hill

The Mad Scientist

There was a scientist called Louise. She made a potion. It made your nails grow. Louise was having a cup of tea, she dropped it. She didn't know it went in the potion. Louise tested it, she had no nails! She made another one then she was back to normal.

Shannon Paulsen (10)
Southway Junior School, Burgess Hill

The Marshmallow Man

Once there was a marshmallow man that liked to take over the world, once he was even in Burgess Hill! He was walking around aimlessly destroying everything. People were running round in circles screaming. People were lighting sticks and poking him hard, he melted and they ate him all up!

Alice Dawes (10)
Southway Junior School, Burgess Hill

My Ball

Sprout and Nemo decided to play 'it'. Then out of the blue Nemo shouted, 'Sprout, you stole my ball!'
'No I didn't you dirty liar!' yelled Sprout.
'What is going on here?' Mum asked.
'Sprout stole my ball and I need it!'
'You don't need a ball to play 'it'!'

Jennifer David (10)
Southway Junior School, Burgess Hill

TARDIS Trouble

The Doctor is flying the TARDIS along the time vortex when suddenly the TARDIS crashes on Mars in the year 100,000 AD. 'I'm going to need to work fast if I want to survive,' so the Doctor worked and worked until he was flying again.

Sam Gething (10)
Southway Junior School, Burgess Hill

Tiny Tales Southern England

Saturday

Hannah woke up, got dressed and walked to school. When she arrived there she looked around. Nobody was there, the door was locked. She checked her watch to see if she was early, she wasn't. She waited ten minutes, still no one came.
Then she realised it was Saturday!

Bethany Cox (10)
Southway Junior School, Burgess Hill

The Pretty Princess And The Frog

A pretty princess rides a horse on an enchanted road. She finds a frog, it asks for a kiss to live, so she does. A handsome prince appears, the prince asks for her to marry him, she says yes. They live happily ever after and have millions of frogs.

Rebecca Davess (10)
Southway Junior School, Burgess Hill

Tiny Tales Southern England

Seaside Adventure

One summer's day Leanne went to the sparkling sea and jumped straight in. She caught a pink jellyfish then she saw something. She swam for her life, it was a shark! She wasn't fast enough, all in one go he ate her up.

Sally Gardiner (9)
Southway Junior School, Burgess Hill

The Eye

Imogen and Oliver went to the river. Imogen was cartwheeling while Oliver was fishing. Then he saw an eye. 'Imogen,' he cried. Imogen came running down the hill. 'Look, there's a crocodile!' he cried. Imogen snatched the fishing net and scooped up the crocodile but it was only a ball!

Imogen Wilson (10)
Southway Junior School, Burgess Hill

The Shipwreck

'Twenty knots already,' cried John.
'Look at that wave,' said Jordan.
'Wow, wow!' shouted Tom. 'What's that over there?" said Tom.
'Let's go and have a look,' said John.'
'Bet you 10 quid it's a monster,' said Tom.
'No monster,' said John, 'just a shipwreck.'
'Hand over the cash mate,' said Tom.

Tom Jenkins (10)
Southway Junior School, Burgess Hill

Ferocious Fire

My heart was pounding at the speed of light. What was happening? Our house was catching fire! It was the hottest day of the year, there was no escape, all the doors, telephones and windows were surrounded by fire, what could I do? There was no escape, please *help me!*

Matthew Carpenter (11)
Southway Junior School, Burgess Hill

Tiny Tales Southern England

King Of Pies

There once was a greedy king who really liked pie. Although he liked the food, he hated the maths. One day he ate too many pies - sixteen to be precise. His stomach bubbled and roared. He grabbed yet another pie, but then … *bang!* The king's tummy exploded into many pieces.

Jacob Instone-Brewer (11)
Southway Junior School, Burgess Hill

Untitled

Once upon a time there was a man that claimed he could run faster than light, no one believed him! He decided to run to the circus. Now he's a freak because he can run so fast. Everyone laughed at him. Everybody lived happily ever after. (Apart from him who's sad).

Austin Golding (11)
Southway Junior School, Burgess Hill

Lunar Simon

'Three, two, one, blast-off!' said the man in the control room. Later that day they were on the moon.

'Amazing!' said Simon in astonishment. After having a look around, they got back in their ship and went home.

Ben McCreadie (10)
Southway Junior School, Burgess Hill

Twist Of Snow White

Snow White had a wicked stepsister. She ran away and met seven creatures. Her mean stepsister gave her a poisonous apple and Snow White fell unconscious. A handsome prince came, then ran away - he thought Snow White was ugly. He lived in a castle with the stepsister.

Connie Pattison (11)
Southway Junior School, Burgess Hill

Deadly Adventure

I decided to take the most deadly adventure ever, I tripped and broke my arm, I screamed at the top of my voice, finally I made it, I wish my stairs were less ignorant and steep, I sat there hitting myself with frustration, damn, for some reason I hate you.

Luke Wilson (11)
Southway Junior School, Burgess Hill

The Sea Creature

Kelly was sailing along and was eating lunch. She suddenly saw something in the water. She screamed! After, she realised it was the Loch Ness monster of Scotland. Soon the police came and investigated the sea. Meanwhile, the monster swallowed her up. She was never seen ever again.

Kate Abercromby (10)
Southway Junior School, Burgess Hill

A Wonderful World

The horse in the field tossed his head, like he had once done when he was young. He had grown up to be such a magnificent stallion. It was evening, the pink sky was a calming thing to look at. Something wonderful happened … a foal to love and care for!

Claire Oldacre (10)
Southway Junior School, Burgess Hill

Escape Of The Cows

One rainy day two cows called Tilly and Daisy were munching on lush green grass. Suddenly there were bolts of lightning, it broke part of the fence in the field. The cows were eager to see what was in the field beyond the fence, so they set off.

Aby Blake (11)
Southway Junior School, Burgess Hill

Tiny Tales Southern England

Disaster Happens

One wet miserable day nine little sheep were sheltering under a tree, when suddenly the huge oak tree fell on top of the sheep. Frantically firefighters took the huge tree off the sheep. They shelter under a different oak tree now.

Lucy Bennet (11)
Southway Junior School, Burgess Hill

The Three Pigs

Once upon a time, there were three little pigs and they built three little houses made of hay, sticks and bricks. Suddenly, a wolf appeared and blew all the houses down, unfortunately the wolf cooked all three pigs on the BBQ.

Chloe Woodall (11)
Southway Junior School, Burgess Hill

When I Went Upstairs

The spooky staircase never ended. I felt like I was going to save a princess from a tower. Suddenly there was a movement, was it the dragon?
Luckily it was just my teddy bear falling off my bed!

Scarlett Secrett (9)
Southway Junior School, Burgess Hill

Life Of A Football

I hate being a football. This thing that gets thrown and pelted about. I don't even get a break. It's good that I'm flat now.

Lewis Pontremoli (9)
Southway Junior School, Burgess Hill

My Fright At ...

I looked out my window. Suddenly I saw a flash. I thought it was a helicopter. I called for my mum. My door was locked so I couldn't get out. My window was open, it floated in. I realised it was a bomb. I picked it up and *bang!* Explosion.

Elizabeth Noble (8)
Southway Junior School, Burgess Hill

Unexplained Mysteries

On a normal day a boy went down to a river with a horrible monster in it. The monster jumped up and ate him alive. People saw, they got police and guns in a battle, they shot it down dead. It was the Loch Ness Monster, now dead. *Blood everywhere!*

Matthew Thoburn (9)
Southway Junior School, Burgess Hill

Shadow Surprise

I lay in one corner of the room because I kept seeing shadows run past me. I started to creep along the floor, keeping as low as I could, but then it jumped out at me … it was my cat Tommy!
I wish I wasn't scared of cat shadows.

Hayley Richardson (9)
Southway Junior School, Burgess Hill

Death Is Not Good

Bang, bang! What was that? *Bang!* It came from over there. *Bang! Argh,* somebody died! *Bang, bang!* Blood was everywhere.
Nee-naw, nee-naw, nee-naw, the police and an ambulance arrived.
Bang, bang! Get him. No you don't! *Bang, bang! Argh!* Everybody died in the PS2 game.

Sam Griffin (9)
Southway Junior School, Burgess Hill

Chad's Race

The gate was scary for Chad. The gate opened, Chad galloped away. A couple of laps after she started to slow down. She was determined to win. She quickly got her breath back and she ran very fast. She was there, first place. She won the race. Wow, that's amazing.

Ellie Hopwood (9)
Southway Junior School, Burgess Hill

The Monster

One morning a baby called Max saw a wicked monster on the ceiling. It was a big rectangle making roaring noises, then it started to shake. The monster was grey with holes in the front of it. When Max was older he found it was an air conditioning machine.

Jason Barrett (9)
Southway Junior School, Burgess Hill

Tiny Tales Southern England

The Unicorn

I looked out of my window, suddenly I saw a flash. Then I saw this huge horse in my back garden, but it didn't look like a horse. It had huge wings and a twirling horn and it was pure white. I went to tell my mum. It had gone.

Rachel Carter (9)
Southway Junior School, Burgess Hill

The Snake

It was coming closer. The snake! Lily cowered back into the grass. She lay on the floor, she hoped she had a chance, a very small one against the snake. The snake was there! She pounced and dug her claws into the snake's slimy skin. Tiger's dinner, cobra delight!

Vicky Lee (10)
Southway Junior School, Burgess Hill

The Prank

Hamish was out fishing when he saw something cutting through the water. He fainted. When he woke up, to his surprise it was still there. Hold on a minute, it seemed to be breaking apart. Finally he saw it was Douglas. Oh Douglas you cheeky little prankster. *Tee-hee!*

Charlie Jones (10)
Southway Junior School, Burgess Hill

The Spider

Lucy opened the door. It was dark. She saw a massive blob in the hallway. Lucy put the light on. *Spider!* It was coming towards her. She was petrified. It started breaking apart. She picked it up and found out her little brother had tricked her with an electric spider!

Anna-Louise Harris (10)
Southway Junior School, Burgess Hill

Tiny Tales Southern England

Huge Creature

Izzie was playing in her garden in the paddling pool. She lived near the boats and sea. Suddenly she saw a huge creature, she ran as fast as she could, trying not to bump into anything. Then she realised, it was a pretend creature on a boat.

Georgia Holloway (10)
Southway Junior School, Burgess Hill

The Ghost

What was that? Jamie thought he heard a ghost. He turned but nothing was there. Jamie's tummy tightened, his spine tingled, heart raced! Jamie froze, hands shaking, he wanted to scream but he couldn't. Jamie was so scared he stood there, the door creaked open … in scampered Jess, his cat.

Isabel Trott (9)
Southway Junior School, Burgess Hill

Hamish

Hamish was walking along a bridge over Loch Ness when he saw a hump sinking into the water. He dived in, thinking it was a hoax. He swam to where the hump had disappeared. Suddenly, teeth as big as icebergs surrounded him and he was never seen again.

Alex Gregory (10)
Southway Junior School, Burgess Hill

Hickery Dickory ...

Mouse clambers up a clock, gets to the top and closes his eyes. *Ding-dong* the clock struck one, the rhyme went wrong, he was up a tree, *ouch!* He fell down. Waiting, mouth open, at the end was Lion wanting his dinner, now it was the end, hickory dickory ...

Ellie Powell (10)
Southway Junior School, Burgess Hill

Tiny Tales Southern England

The Green Hand

It was coming, a monster, closer and closer!
Tom was scared, he froze then shouted, a hand reached out. *Argh!*
Then Tom realised it was just his sister home from a fancy dress party.

Tommy King (10)
Southway Junior School, Burgess Hill

Wonderland Comes To An End

Sora felt he was falling from the sky but he landed on ground safely. He saw lots of doors and he went through them. Once he went through the sleepy door Sora's squirrel was in the queen's castle. He took and saved Alice and let her come along with him.

Harry Woolven (9)
Southway Junior School, Burgess Hill

On The Beach

One day Grace was in the grimy water, she swam into the deep, there was a pitch-black hole at the bottom. She was splashing like mad, suddenly a snap at her leg, her brother came up from the bottom, 'Fooled you,' he said. Grace was crying for one hour.

Molly Dennett-Thorpe (8)
Southway Junior School, Burgess Hill

That Night

That one night, about 8pm, a girl looked out her window, it was a full moon at 9pm. She looked back out but something was not right. Something was covering the moon, what was it? She ran downstairs to her mum and dad, the mystery was unsolved.

Sarah Owen (9)
Southway Junior School, Burgess Hill

Untitled

Today was the day, the cup final, only 10 players were left. The game started, it was 10 minutes each way. We played the whole match, it went into extra time. That was 5 minutes each way. We played the half. In the last minute we scored, *yes!*

George Brown
Southway Junior School, Burgess Hill

Bugs

Ann creaked open the huge door, she was in a dark room. She lit a match … there were bugs everywhere! On the walls, ceiling and stairs and even in her shoes! She had a lifelong fear of spiders … there were more spiders than ever! She was scared to death!

Isobel Penfold (8)
Southway Junior School, Burgess Hill

The Dinosaur Friendship

Some dinosaurs made friends and shared fair and square. A million years ago Tyrannosaurus-Tom was starving. He saw a carcass of a sauropod. But Allow-Jack was going for it too. They fought for two hours then they decided to split it fifty-fifty and they made friends forever.

Ryan Sandall (9)
Southway Junior School, Burgess Hill

The Talking Toothbrushes

There once lived Ellie and Emily the talking toothbrushes.
Once Molly the toothpaste knocked them down so they got revenge by trying to wash her out but she's unbeatable, but the toothpaste had fear of humans' mouths so they waited. Suddenly a human came and they never saw Molly again.

Emily Baxter (9)
Southway Junior School, Burgess Hill

How Embarrassing

I was there, it happened to me, who would ever think it would, I wet myself. How embarrassing, I felt like never going out again. Even my best friend was laughing at me. Why couldn't it happen to Conner or Ellie instead of me! Just why did it happen?

Emily Sayers (9)
Southway Junior School, Burgess Hill

No One Here

I crept up in the dark attic, my hands were sweating. I heard a chuckle! 'Oh no!' I saw a black shadowed object walk past. I wanted to go back but I had to discover more ... I screamed at that very moment!
I suddenly realised it was my ... sister! *Weird!*

Leah Walden (9)
Southway Junior School, Burgess Hill

Stage Fright

Easy. My stomach twisted and turned. Slowly, my legs began to feel like jelly. 'Argh … ! When is this going to end?'
Without warning, my head began to throb. I looked down at my feet, took a deep breath and left the stage, clutching the trophy. It was horrible!

Julia Phillips (11)
Southway Junior School, Burgess Hill

Silence

The hallway seemed to continue forever. There was silence behind me, silence in front, silence all around. *Bang!* What was that? This is ludicrous. Me being scared. Suddenly I heard another noise.
'Surprise!'
That was the best birthday party I ever had.

Jessica Manley (11)
Southway Junior School, Burgess Hill

Tiny Tales Southern England

Katie And The Dragon

She was trapped. 'Help, I'm trapped!' Katie only had a little bit of air when … *smash!* A glider heard her call. She clambered on his back and flew away. Katie had a new best friend. Katie's mum loved the glider too! They lived happily for many years.

Shannon Webb (11)
Southway Junior School, Burgess Hill

Locks

Locked. Kayla kept tugging the key. The door, which wouldn't open, was stuck - forever. Silently Kayla turned around as quickly as possible. Footsteps were stumbling round the corner; haunting her. A familiar voice approached.

'Kayla I've changed the locks,' her mum's voice reassured her. There were no monsters … anymore!

Katherine Roberts
Southway Junior School, Burgess Hill

Tiny Tales Southern England

Horse Trip

At the first sight of a horse I ran away … petrified. Carla, my best friend invited me to her horse riding party. Nervously I went. Luckily my courage took over. I was about the same height as a horse. Since then I have won medals and ride every day.

Alexandra Pattenden (10)
Southway Junior School, Burgess Hill

Elf Attack

George helped Jamie board up the windows - they were under attack from the magical time travelling elves. Suddenly, one of their evil opponents shot through the ancient Chinese window and hit George in the eye. Luckily, Richard Nixon Junior teleported to his side, cured his eye and killed the elves.

Connor Glaze (11)
Southway Junior School, Burgess Hill

The Chase

Darren and I were running, the wolfman hot on our heels. We reached a barn. Darren leapt onto its wooden rafters. I tried several attempts, where all ineffective, to grasp the beams. Then sighed and looked the beast in the eye. I felt its fangs pierce my flesh, then …

Lewis Walker (11)
Southway Junior School, Burgess Hill

A Fairy And Her House

There was a fairy, who had a broken house, she couldn't afford a new one so that's what Tinkerbell lived in. She didn't think anyone knew. She took a stroll in the woods one day. When she came home, there was a new house in its place. Who built it?

Maria Romer (11)
Southway Junior School, Burgess Hill

Humpty Dumpty

Humpty Dumpty who was sitting (as usual) on his hard stone garden wall, was stroking his shiny bald egg head. Suddenly he fell off. He didn't get bruised, he didn't get bumped. No king's horses or king's men came to put Humpty together again. In fact Humpty Dumpty bungee jumped.

Kathryn Tidbury
Southway Junior School, Burgess Hill

The Black Creeper

The steps creaked. Something black, thin and with pointy ears was coming down! 'I wonder what that is, it's a little spooky,' I whispered. The face came out and it looked friendly. The reason it creaked was the broken stair! I realised it was my cat Fefe!

Georgia Vigar (8)
Southway Junior School, Burgess Hill

Tiny Tales Southern England

Goldilocks And The Three Bears

'I'm tired,' yawned Goldilocks. So she went upstairs and had a snooze.
Then the three bears came back and saw Goldilocks in Baby Bear's bed. 'What's going on?' shrieked Baby Bear.
So Goldilocks said, 'I just want to play.'
The bears listened and replied, 'OK then!'
So Goldilocks played happily.

Lucy Jellett (8)
Southway Junior School, Burgess Hill

Little Red Riding Hood

Little Red Riding Hood went through the forest to go and give her granny some biscuits. However, something was in the trees, moving about. She ran as quickly as a cheetah. She found her granny's cottage and went inside. Kindly she gave her granny the biscuits.
'Thanks my dear.'

Shannon Smith (7)
Southway Junior School, Burgess Hill

My Goal Against Marle Place

My goal against Marle Place is a memory. It was like this; Jack played a corner in, and it fell to me. I used my left foot to kick it in the net. My celebration was running to my manager who was across the pitch, I also kissed the badge.

Sam Rattle (8)
Southway Junior School, Burgess Hill

Snow White And The Seven Aliens

One night Snow White saw a light outside her window. She looked outside and gasped. There were seven aliens. The aliens took one look at her then they got back into the spaceship and flew away. She got up the next day and found them camping on her lawn.

Saffron Revell (8)
Southway Junior School, Burgess Hill

The Mystical Bird

One day I was happily playing with my little brother when he started crying for no reason. I was thinking, *what is he crying about?* Then I saw a mystical bird in the sky. I tried to chase it but it flew away, I'll never forget it.

Jamie Bareham (8)
Southway Junior School, Burgess Hill

Humpty Dumpty

One day Humpty Dumpty sat on a castle wall.
Suddenly the king spotted him and bellowed,
'Get that giant egg off my wall!'
'OK,' replied two voices.
So they climbed up the wall and pushed him off! He landed with a splat. But unfortunately he could not be fixed.

Cameron Beattie (8)
Southway Junior School, Burgess Hill

My Dream

I sat there waiting for my fear to be over, then as if by magic we zoomed faster than anything to the landing. It was scarier than anything in my life, I wish I didn't have a really bad fear of aeroplanes.

Ellie Scott (8)
Southway Junior School, Burgess Hill

Untitled

One day Humpty Dumpty had to do a show in front of his school. He had to do the show all by himself and he had to sing. He went to bed and had a bad dream and then he woke up. The next day he performed his show.

Parmila Manan
Southway Junior School, Burgess Hill

Tiny Tales Southern England

Hell House

Dad had just dropped me at my auntie's, I started to get suspicious. Later I decided to go home to see what was happening. I ran home, when I got there I searched for the key, I found it, I opened the door, Hell was released.

George Clare (9)
Southway Junior School, Burgess Hill

The Mysterious Game

One long lonely day there was a boy and he sat at home bored. So he went to the attic. He brought down a game and when he opened it, out came a lion! It pounced at him and nearly clawed him, it took another swipe and got him. *Argh!*

Courtney Hartfield (9)
Southway Junior School, Burgess Hill

Tiny Tales Southern England

The Boy Who Went Through A Hole

One day a boy goes to school and he goes to sit down on the table. But suddenly he gets sucked into the table through a hole, when it appears. He was so scared. He didn't know what to do. Did he get out or not? I wonder what happened?

Michaela Cartwright-Ormston (9)
Southway Junior School, Burgess Hill

Humpty Dumpty's Ghost

Humpty Dumpty was sitting on the wall licking ice cream one night. Suddenly he heard a scary voice, it sounded like a ghost, he went closer but he couldn't see anything, he turned around and he saw a ghost, it took the sheet off, it was just his friend.

Sophie Ackland (9)
Southway Junior School, Burgess Hill

Tiny Tales Southern England

The Surprise Fall

When Lucy arrived home she was surprised, everything was a mess, her mum and dad were not home, there was a creak, her door flew open. 'Surprise! Happy birthday Lucy.'
'Argh!'

Leah Batson Jenner (9)
Southway Junior School, Burgess Hill

The Naughty Baby

Once I was asked if I would like to babysit, I said yes so I went over there and the house was so tidy, but that's when the trouble came. The baby made the house a mess, I had to tidy it up, then I sat down.

Georgina Owen (8)
Southway Junior School, Burgess Hill

Anne Boleyn

Only just escaped from Auntie. It's lovely and cool by the river here at Hever Castle. *'Argh!'* A figure comes gliding over the water towards me. Help! Glittering from head to toe in sparkly jewels. Anne Boleyn?
I wake up, my head spinning. A dream possibly?

Ellie Parker (10)
Southway Junior School, Burgess Hill

The Toothpaste Excuse

'I squeezed the toothpaste out too hard, you can ask my parents if you like.'
Ring! 'I see, I'll let you off this time!'
Phew! I do wish I went to school at my own planet and wasn't an alien from space, then I wouldn't be late for school!

Charlotte Bates (9)
Southway Junior School, Burgess Hill

Untitled

One day Captain Conner bought a new ship, he sailed off. Then he saw Blackbeard had catapults in his boat, but Conner's was just a pink ship.
5 hours later they had a sword fight and Captain Conner stabbed Blackbeard. They sailed off to Catapult Island.

Benjamin House (9)
Southway Junior School, Burgess Hill

Untitled

The ground was shaking, everyone was screaming. I was hanging on to my dog. It was an earthquake. We all looked out the window, there were giant cracks in the ground, cars, trains, shops, buses and motorbikes, a few big houses all broken.
After a few minutes it was over.

David Sadler (9)
Southway Junior School, Burgess Hill

Tiny Tales Southern England

Scares

She walked cautiously into the dark, eerie wood. She started to run faster, faster, landed on dried red stuff. She screamed. Then she saw it, a big, vicious, man-eating thing. She tried to run but something had got her foot. She pulled. It didn't come. *Bam!* She was gone.

Jude Michie (9)
Talavera Junior School, Aldershot

The Wood

She took a small breath and stopped. She heard something like bones cracking, it could be a spirit skeleton and then suddenly she saw something run in front of her, she ran as fast as she could but she tripped and then she felt a bony hand on her shoulder …

Katie Robson (7)
Talavera Junior School, Aldershot

Untitled

The woods were dark and cold, she stopped to look. She saw orange eyes. She was still like a statue. She slowly moved as she was scared. Something got her leg. It was green and long. She pulled it out and ran, fast as she could. She was safe.

Bindu Thapa (8)
Talavera Junior School, Aldershot

On A Dark And Spooky Night

She entered the dark, spooky woods. The hair on the back of her neck prickled and footsteps followed behind her. She slowly turned around. There was no one there. She stopped. She was frightened. The footsteps got closer. It got to the light. It was Mum coming to take her home.

Kiya Brown (8)
Talavera Junior School, Aldershot

Untitled

It was a dark, spooky wood. He heard something from the rustling bushes. *Snap!* He turned slowly, he heard another *snap!* It came from the tree. He stopped. He saw evil yellow eyes, killer teeth. It backed away. Suddenly it came running. The beast was revealed. It was a wolf.

Lloyd McCarthy (9)
Talavera Junior School, Aldershot

Untitled

In the deep, dark woods he heard a noise. It was a strange noise. He thought it was his tummy because it was shaking. Then he crept in case there were any monsters. Suddenly he saw some eyes peeking in the bush. He was frightened. He ran home shouting, 'Mum!'

Ben Colvin (8)
Talavera Junior School, Aldershot

The Beast

The wood was dark and creepy. She trembled as she tiptoed through the tall trees. She froze. She heard something crack and footsteps nearby, she turned around and saw yellow eyes. It was hairy, tall. She got caught. It tore her apart, that was the end of the girl.

Thomas Askey (8)
Talavera Junior School, Aldershot

In The Woods

She entered the deep, dark woods. She could hear rustling leaves behind her. She was very scared, she wondered what it was. Was it footsteps? She stopped, she looked. Yellow eyes were everywhere. They came closer. She could hear sharp, snarling teeth. She ran deeper into the woods.

Annie Davies (8)
Talavera Junior School, Aldershot

Tiny Tales Southern England

Untitled

The woods were big and spooky and very dark. She slowly looked around. She slowly spun round, she saw big red eyes. She did not know what it was. She heard it growl, she ran away fast. It was coming and she looked behind her. It was a zombie man!

Billy Gilfilan (8)
Talavera Junior School, Aldershot

The Dark Wood

The wood was spooky and dark. She crept through. She tiptoed along the brown twigs. 'What's that?' she whispered. She saw some yellow glowing eyes. It had grey fur and a very long tail. She stopped and listened. She heard grunting.
It was only her mother with a skipping rope.

Abigail Smith (8)
Talavera Junior School, Aldershot

The Wood Of No Return

She took a large breath and entered. It was dark and creepy. She started to walk slowly. Then she stopped. She span round quickly. She heard a loud noise. She ran to where it was coming from. Then she stopped again. Something was coming. It had large, white, pointy teeth.

Tyler Duckworth (9)
Talavera Junior School, Aldershot

The Wood Of No Return

He entered the deep wood. He stopped. What could he see? It was red evil eyes. His hairs stood up on his back. It licked its lips. He ran as fast as he could. He tripped. The bear stomped to him and gobbled him up. No one saw him again.

Samuel Cresswell (9)
Talavera Junior School, Aldershot

The Spooks' Wood

She took a large breath and entered. It was spooky and dark. She could hear twigs snapping, owls swooping, she could see eyes red, yellow, blue and pink, she was scared. She stopped. She turned around. It had thick hairs, burly eyes, huge belly and giant feet, it was Mum.

Amy Rose (9)
Talavera Junior School, Aldershot

Spooky Forest

He took a look around and entered the spooky, gloomy woods. Suddenly he heard a giant roar. He froze like an ice cube. He heard a rumble. He ran quickly but was too late. He saw it, a flesh-eating beast. He ran from the beast as fast as lightning.

Thomas Clarkson (7)
Talavera Junior School, Aldershot

Tiny Tales Southern England

Spooky Boat

At night we were asleep, there were noises outside. They got closer and closer until the thing started to say my name louder and louder. It broke the end off the boat and the boat started to sink faster and faster. The dead captain was driving the boat.

Brendan Kane (8)
Talavera Junior School, Aldershot

The Vampire

Alex was walking around the boat, she heard a scream. It was so creepy that she couldn't move. She heard footsteps. They came louder and louder until she was face to face with a vampire. The vampire had killed the captain. She couldn't see anything. She dived into the sea.

Alex Laken (8)
Talavera Junior School, Aldershot

Tiny Tales Southern England

The Creepy Wood

The wood was creepy and very dark. He stopped. He heard something like rustling leaves. It came closer. The hairs on the back of his neck prickled. He climbed a tree and looked, sharp teeth like daggers. He fell off the tree and ran for his life.

Joseph Rowles (9)
Talavera Junior School, Aldershot

Untitled

She saw a big branch. She heard a loud noise and she ran to her house. She saw the sharp teeth and yellow face come to her window. She opened the door and turned around. There was nobody there. Her mum came in from the bus stop.

Nicole Oakley (9)
Talavera Junior School, Aldershot

Untitled

One night a boy called Sam ran in the wood and got lost. He walked in the wood and heard footsteps behind him. He stopped and looked. Nothing was there. Sam carried on walking through the creepy wood. He reached the end and ran to his house. He was safe.

Yetnam Limbu (8)
Talavera Junior School, Aldershot

In The Woods

She entered the dark spooky forest. She heard a strange noise coming from in front of her. She became frightened. She kept walking, the hairs on the back of her neck prickled. Then she was faced with a monster wearing a cloak before her. She screamed. She started to run …

Leena Cobb (9)
Talavera Junior School, Aldershot

Untitled

One night there was a pitch-black night and it was noisy in the wood; there was rattling and banging but there were also some leaves rustling. A wild dog was hunting. Slowly, slowly, he crept forward. *Snap!* Now his children would be fed.

Billie-Jo Churm (8)
Talavera Junior School, Aldershot

Untitled

In a dark, dark wood it was very horrid and dark, spooky and cold. The trees were dying. The leaves were falling off the trees, branches were breaking and the lightning was striking. The thunder had struck again and the trees were very swashy and snappy.

Lewis Totterdell (8)
Talavera Junior School, Aldershot

Untitled

It was a very gloomy night. The rustle of the dead leaves shocked the nightly animals and creatures as they walked over them. The trees creaked and branches snapped. The spooky wind made whistling noises around the trees and through windows of old crooked houses.

Millie Thomas (7)
Talavera Junior School, Aldershot

Untitled

In the dark wood there is loud thunder and flashing lightning. The thunder goes *bang, bang, bang!* The branches sweep and creak, sweep and creak. Then the noise gets louder and scarier. The leaves on the branches are waving. Then they keep on falling down loudly.

Callum Waters (8)
Talavera Junior School, Aldershot

Untitled

In a dark wood, on a dark night all is silent. You can only hear the animals hunting. The dead leaves and the branches are creaking. No one can see the moon because the moon is covered by the black cloud. Suddenly he comes to a clearing. All is peaceful.

Diya Gurung (8)
Talavera Junior School, Aldershot

The Shock

One night I was trembling in my bed. It was a cold, foggy night. The wind flowed across me. I heard a sound. *Oooh!* It was a scary sound, I was scared, I crept to the window shaking. I looked up, then I looked down. I shook, what was it?

Harry Prescott (8)
Velmead Junior School, Fleet

The Spinning Ride

My head was dizzy. My feet were weak. My tummy felt funny. My head fell forwards. I opened my eyes, I saw things spinning. I could not see Mum or Dad. I felt as if I bumped my head. Everything stopped spinning. I was on a spinning merry-go-round.

Neve Mills (8)
Velmead Junior School, Fleet

My Ride

I was going up and up. I held my breath, I couldn't take it. The cranking got quieter and quieter. I was getting to the top. Oh no! I was at the top, it stopped. I closed my eyes, I went down, I was too scared to scream! It's over.

Lauren Pocock (8)
Velmead Junior School, Fleet

A Wicked Spell

My brother and I were trapped. A witch and a wizard had turned my mum and dad evil. They had made them put us into the pot just like they did to my mum and dad. I wished for help. Help came instantly. A wizard came and saved the day!

Abigail Larkin (8)
Velmead Junior School, Fleet

On Holiday

One sunny day we set off on holiday. We jumped in the car and drove off. We were very excited. Suddenly Mum remembered we had forgotten a suitcase. So we turned around. Dad was grumpy! Finally we arrived at the hotel. Later Mum realised we had forgotten our pyjamas. *Whoops!*

Louise King (8)
Velmead Junior School, Fleet

Tiny Tales Southern England

The Rocket

Finally the last of them were on the launch pad. Someone shouted, 'Launch off!' much too soon. Anyway at least they went off. An hour later there was a huge explosion. To our amazement it landed right on its target, London.

Peter Wilkins
Velmead Junior School, Fleet

Time Travel

I bought a watch, I changed the time, *where was I?* I wondered, it appeared that it was 2051. The cars were flying everywhere. Everyone laughed because of how I was dressed. Everything was silver and gold. The cars had big engines. I got home and played PS2 games.

Jack Pearce (8)
Velmead Junior School, Fleet

My Haunted House

I went downstairs in the middle of the night and I saw a ghost.
'Mum! Mum! There's a ghost in my room. Mum let's get out!'
Suddenly the whole house came to life. The ghost was chasing me around the house. I ran away.

Ella Hurst (8)
Velmead Junior School, Fleet

The Fight

Harry and Voldemort were fighting in the graveyard trying to kill each other. It went one way then the other. It was tight. Suddenly, *bang!* Harry went running into the portkey. He was back and had won the triwizard cup. But Cedric Diggory was dead. Harry started to cry sadly.

Jake Wish (8)
Velmead Junior School, Fleet

A Frightening Journey

I fell asleep. When I woke up my stomach flipped. I said to Mum, 'I think I am going to be ill,' so I dashed to the bathroom, but halfway there I fell to the ground and I was sick. Abi had used her potion kit on me.

Sophie Hayes (8)
Velmead Junior School, Fleet

A Crash On The M5

One day there was a crash on the M5. He was on the wrong side of the road. *'Move out the way!'* He skidded and then a motorbike crashed into the car. Two more cars crashed and then the air bag came out. Somebody called the ambulance.

Scott Newstead (7)
Velmead Junior School, Fleet

Tiny Tales Southern England

Super Dog

It was a dark night. Everybody was asleep except Super Dog. Super Dog is a good dog. He saves people every ten minutes. One day he heard a knock on his kennel, it was a man in trouble, 'Help! Help!' said the man. 'I am in danger. I'm dying. Help!'

Jessica Staker (8)
Velmead Junior School, Fleet

Boy In Car Accident

One day there was a boy walking across the road. Suddenly a car came soaring round the corner. It couldn't stop. It skidded into the boy. The next day the boy woke up in hospital. They had to do a serious operation which hurt very much. He survived.

Simon Malley (8)
Velmead Junior School, Fleet

My Puppy

My puppy is called Toby. We bought him from a woman that lived in a flat. I thought he was going to be vicious but he was cute. We went to our house and showed him around his home. We bought him loads of toys and a comfortable bed.

Victoria Driscoll (8)
Velmead Junior School, Fleet

The Wizard And The Gingerbread Man

One day in an old castle a wizard was casting a spell on a gingerbread man but he went wrong. 'Bye!' said the gingerbread man and jumped out the window. He soon came to a sweet shop and jumped onto the gingerbread shelf but a boy saw him and *munch!*

Miles Wheway (9)
Velmead Junior School, Fleet

The Wrong Spell

There lived a wizard who helped people. Two miles away from him lived a young boy who longed for a pet. He walked two miles to see the wizard. Finally he made it and asked for a pet. Then all of a sudden he cast a spell on the boy.

Kailey Driscoll (9)
Velmead Junior School, Fleet

The Great Race

Tom gets into his car. He is starting to get ready for the great race.
'Ready, steady, go!'
Tom races down the hill, over the bridge. He is now third! He is racing for the title. The racing title. He is now second, now first, he is going to win!

Christopher Altini (9)
Velmead Junior School, Fleet

The Champion Swimmer

I dive in, I'm first to lead, someone comes behind me but I speed on, no one near me now, I'm still in the lead. Someone tying with me, about halfway to the finish line, I'm nearly there, just a few more metres. I'm slightly ahead, so close, I win!

Ross Newman (9)
Velmead Junior School, Fleet

The Egyptian Mummies

On a dark spooky night in Egypt four mummies came alive and started approaching people and kidnapped them. The mummies dragged the people into their tombs. All of a sudden you heard the loudest shriek you have ever heard because the people were turned into mummies.

Matthew Lockett (9)
Velmead Junior School, Fleet

The Return Of Super Sophie

Argh! screamed Bethany. It was seconds away from impact, she was scared. Then she heard a drumming sound on the left. Then around the corner came Super Sophie! Bethany shouted, 'Over here!' yet there was ten seconds left, nine

…

'Sophie, time to wake up.' Was that a dream?

Isobel Dudfield (9)
Velmead Junior School, Fleet

What Will Happen Next?

The sun shone on the blue sea. The Mary Rose swayed side to side, just outside the coast of Britain. As the ship's ropes untied, the Mary Rose set off down the water. Twenty-four miles from the land the Mary Rose turned, but no one knows what happened next.

Olivia Close (10)
Velmead Junior School, Fleet

Racing Down The Hill

I was on top of the slide on the very top of the hill. *Argh!* The brakes fell off! I was speeding down the hill at light speed. *Duck!* Now that was close. Oh no! A rock! It sent me flying in the air.
Bang! Ouch! Phew! Now that's finished.

Callum Gooding (8)
Velmead Junior School, Fleet

Humpty Dumpty

Humpty Dumpty lived in a peach, but the peach was too soft. Humpty Dumpty lived in an apple, but the apple was too hard. Humpty Dumpty lived in a pineapple but the pineapple was too spiky. Humpty Dumpty lived in a box and the box was just right.

Brittany Pepper
Velmead Junior School, Fleet

Alien

Tsseww! Tsseww! The sound of lasers filled the air around me. *Tsseww! Tsseww!* I raced round the corner. I slipped. A cold, slimy thing leapt on me. I turned my head.
There was my brother holding a toy laser gun.

Alexander Medler
Velmead Junior School, Fleet

Car Park

'Come on, keep up.' *Bang! Crash!* 'We need to run like the wind.' Eventually we reached our destination. Dad looked at his watch. *'Nnnoooo! Our parking ticket ran out!'*

Dominic Abbott
Velmead Junior School, Fleet

The Chase

I was running as fast as I could, chasing after the deadly hound. It was getting away, this was my last and only chance to get it, it was escaping from the graveyard into the darkness! I had just missed the train! Now how would I get there?

Will Jones (10)
Velmead Junior School, Fleet

Strike

Marco is so cute in his PE kit. I gaze at him until Sarah throws a basketball at me and giggles with her gang! She's been bullying me ever since Year 3. But I am so getting her back! I pick up the ball and I chuck it! *Victory!*

Emma Harber (10)
Velmead Junior School, Fleet

The Thing

I waited in a place of misery and despair, undetected for now.
'Next,' said the thing.
I stumbled into the room and was strapped into a chair. Suddenly a mind-blowing sound. A drill-like weapon. Then the dentist asked me if I was okay. Phew, it was all over.

James Galbraith (11)
Velmead Junior School, Fleet

Harmful? Healer?

He's coming. Will he heal me or decide I'm better off dead? He dissects people. He's here. I fear him, loathe him. He may make me better or only able to make me live longer. They have sharp objects that may be used on me or against me. The doctor …

Adam Russell (11)
Velmead Junior School, Fleet

I'm Late!

I was going down the dark, spooky corridor, the floorboards creaked, I heard something coming from behind me! It was only a mouse, but then in front of me a door opened ... It was hideous, it was my teacher telling me that I was late for class.

Phillip Chorlton (11)
Velmead Junior School, Fleet

The Fox And The Crow

One day there was a hungry fox. He was no ordinary fox. He was cunning. He saw a crow eating bread. He said, 'Crow, you have a beautiful voice.'
'Thank you.'
'Please can you sing?'
The crow started singing, the bread dropped and the fox took it and ran far.

Vrushangan Sumanoharan (11)
Velmead Junior School, Fleet

Untitled

High above, looking down on the land I used to know, but now I'm so high it seems so very small. I know this land so very well but now it seems so strange that when I'm up here, I wonder how I ever knew my way. I love flying.

Andrea Goring (11)
Velmead Junior School, Fleet

The Beast

So there I was, the beast coming closer, a thousand tiny voices screaming out at me in my head. The bloodthirsty beast came closer, breathing down my neck, now there was only one chance, one way out, the evacuation was ready, the alarm sounded, I was safe from my teacher.

Robert Snellock (11)
Velmead Junior School, Fleet

The Death I Am Given Every Week

The monster was coming with her messy hair and her bumpy purple skin. Its evil sword poised and she was ready to hand me her deadly weekly torture.
Then the teacher handed me my homework, pen still in her hand and I groaned.

Tom Goodyear (10)
Velmead Junior School, Fleet

The Monster

'No I shall never lower myself, no way, dream on.'
'I'll take away the TV.'
'You monster, you won't do that.'
'I can and I will, now do it.'
'I can't Mum, I hate vegetables.'
'Well then, no TV.'
'No, my life is over, I'm dead forever, goodbye world.'

Alexandra Keenan (11)
Velmead Junior School, Fleet

Smoothie

Constantly spinning round and round - *stop!* Suddenly a huge finger, driving towards us. Twisting, turning like a whirlpool, churning around, juice goes squeezing out! Parts of me flying all over the place, I'm falling apart, screaming inside me. That is how I became a smoothie.

Nadia Hamid (11)
Velmead Junior School, Fleet

The Disappearing Boy

I was sitting in the Easter Islands, when I heard a strange noise like an earthquake. I got up, walked to where the noise was. I saw a boy running away. Suddenly he disappeared, I ran down there - he was gone. I couldn't see him anywhere. He had vanished.

Michael Robinson (11)
Velmead Junior School, Fleet

The Black Wine Cellar

I clambered down the blackening stairs, very nervously. Eventually, I set my foot into the dark wine cellar! A black, luminous shadow was wafting on the walls towards me! I froze in horror, however I couldn't run!
I sighed with relief as Jazz, my cat crept out of the shadows.

James Leggett (11)
Velmead Junior School, Fleet

In My Bedroom

In the jungle with no sight of freedom. The mess on the ground, my bedroom, toys just scattered all over the ground, not knowing where anything is when my mum said, 'Tidy your room.'
I say, 'It's a jungle, can't cut it down on my own.'

Thomas Bee (11)
Velmead Junior School, Fleet

Tiny Tales Southern England

The One Handed Spoctuman

It was Tuesday night, I was in a restaurant, and I saw a bus pull up on the other side of the street. A man showed up with red eyes and a hand of a fork. He walked into the room, it turned out that he was holding a fork.

Jamie Richards (11)
Velmead Junior School, Fleet

Where Am I?

There I was in the middle of nowhere. I was lost, help me get back home.
Ten minutes later I saw a light, I walked towards it. It was a house. I went inside. I shouted, I said, 'Who's here?'
'It's just your mum. No need to worry.'
'OK.'

Jarvis Reay (11)
Velmead Junior School, Fleet

Stormy Seas

The ship was sinking rapidly. Water gushed aboard in every direction, creating scenes of devastation. Towering waves crashed down, consuming all. People jumped for their lives, as the boat finally sank … 'Time for bed,' yelled Mum. Jimmy got out of the bath; his toy boat patted dry for another adventure.

Jolyon Dannatt (10)
West Dean CE Primary School, Chichester

Naughty Children

It was Saturday evening, Tom was babysitting. All seemed quiet until the kids decided they were going to play havoc on him. They tied him to a chair, raided the larder and threw food at him.

Suddenly the parents came back. They gave poor Tom the sack, he was glad.

Robert McCann (11)
West Dean CE Primary School, Chichester

The Three Little Hermit Crabs And The Big Bad Bird

There were three hermit crabs. A bird tried to eat one and crushed the shell but Hermit escaped just in time and joined his friend. The bird also crushed his but they got out and joined the final crab whose shell was strong. The bird couldn't eat them and left.

Theo Ormrod Davis (10)
West Dean CE Primary School, Chichester

The Skiing Accident

My skis crossed as I left the mogul and took to the air, going higher and higher. I landed with my legs twisted in different directions and pain shot through my body. As I looked down, a stream of blood weaved its way through the snow, and I passed out.

Ella Herman (9)
West Dean CE Primary School, Chichester

Tiny Footprints

There were tiny footprints on my bedroom window, where did they come from? I was puzzled, how did they get there? At first I thought the garden gnome had come alive. Then I realised, a little house martin lived under the eaves … oh well, it's good to pretend.

Ollie Dodge (9)
West Dean CE Primary School, Chichester

The Wish

It was heading right for me, I saw my life flash before my eyes. Its headlights were glaring down on me. I scampered away as an ungovernable terror gripped me. I gasped for breath.
I really wish those humans could see us rabbits!

Freya Davies (11)
West Dean CE Primary School, Chichester

The Truth Of Humpty Dumpty

There was an egg called Dumpty, his friends called him Humpty, they say he fell off a wall, but he didn't really at all! He was pushed off, by Prince Laff, and never found again.

Bethan Jerrett (11)
West Dean CE Primary School, Chichester

Bubblegum

Charlotte wanted some bubblegum but wasn't allowed it. She took some money out of her money box and went to the shop. When she got home, her mum was there, Charlotte's mum thought she had been good and treated her to some bubblegum. 'Charlotte, will you own up?'

Louise Cresswell (8)
West Dean CE Primary School, Chichester

My Fear Of …

The ground beneath my feet stood firm, I began to climb. Higher and higher. Eventually I reached the top. I placed my bottom onto the edge, I reached for the sides. I thrust myself forward, down the surface as quickly as I could. How I loved my red slide.

Rebecca Callow (10)
West Dean CE Primary School, Chichester

The Milkman's Revenge

Milkman Fred would daily drive up Bluebell Lane passing some horrid children. They would throw stones at the float to smash bottles. Fred was fed up. He hired an ice cream van and sold ices to the children, sprinkled with nail clippings instead of nuts. They never pestered him again!

Esther King (11)
West Dean CE Primary School, Chichester

Changing!

As I swam through the water, my heart rate doubled. I'd spotted a bottle. Could this be what I needed? Picking it up I swam to the surface and drank from it. My tail changed back into two legs! I was human again, not a mermaid. I felt incredibly wonderful!

Hannah Lyons (10)
West Dean CE Primary School, Chichester

My Moth

Yesterday I found a big moth, I took it in to show Dad who looked it up on the Internet. It was a privet hawk moth. I put it in a fishtank and put it by my light in my bedroom. It kept flying and woke me up.

Luke Ewins (9)
West Dean CE Primary School, Chichester

Information

We hope you have enjoyed reading this book - and that you will continue to enjoy it in the coming years.

If you like reading and writing, drop us a line or give us a call and we'll send you a free information pack. Alternatively visit our website at www.youngwriters.co.uk

Write to:
Young Writers Information,
Remus House,
Coltsfoot Drive,
Peterborough,
PE2 9JX
Tel: (01733) 890066
Email: youngwriters@forwardpress.co.uk